WEALTH WITHOUT WALL STREET

WEALTH WITHOUT WALL STREET

3 STEPS TO
FREEDOM
THROUGH
PASSIVE INCOME

JOEY MURÉ
RUSS MORGAN

Wealth Without Wall Street

3 Steps to Freedom Through Passive Income

First Edition

ISBN 978-1-5445-2447-4 *Hardcover*

978-1-5445-2445-0 *Paperback*

978-1-5445-2446-7 *Ebook*

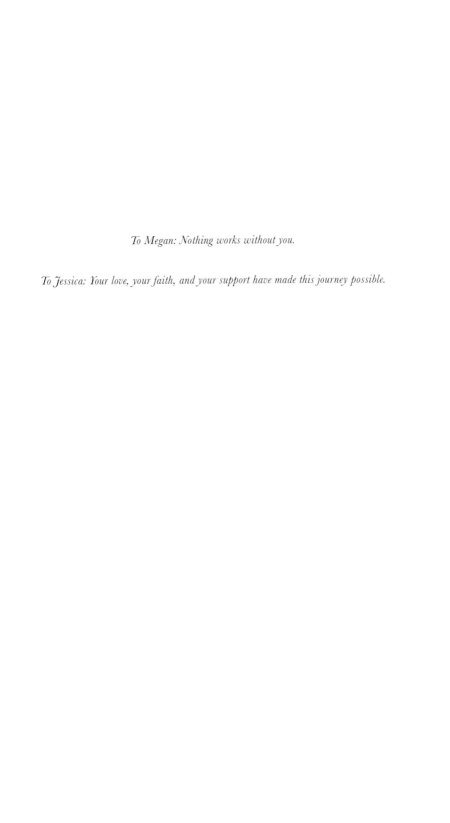

To Megan: Nothing works without you.

To Jessica: Your love, your faith, and your support have made this journey possible.

CONTENTS

PREFACE

You. You are your greatest asset in your quest for Financial Freedom. Investing in you is the best place you could ever put your money. Why? Because God created you for a unique purpose. He created you to reflect Him in all that you do.

Your life is not an accident. You have been given certain resources that no one else has been given. We mean it. The time in which you were born, in the place you were born, the experiences you have been given (whether good or bad), the relationships you have, the time you have right now, the money you make, the money you have in the bank, the career you have—all are gifts you have been entrusted with that no one else has exactly.

Think of it like a fingerprint. All of these resources come together to create your unique world and calling. How you choose to use these resources makes all the difference.

We believe we will give an account for everything that has been entrusted to us. We are caretakers of someone else's property—stewards of God's resources.

The default approach to all of resource management is to

simply react to your surroundings your entire life. Some will follow the herd and, in a sense, turn off their brains and just keep their heads down and hope everything works out in the end. That person would probably never buy this book or reach Financial Freedom. But the fact you are reading this says you are looking to think differently.

The other path is to take the resources entrusted to you and systematically and proactively seek wisdom and guidance on the path to Financial Freedom. Such a person will look to mentors who have been where they want to be. If you are such a person, this book will provide for you a true path to follow to get to Financial Freedom as fast as possible.

The two of us have found that all of life is about loving God and loving people, and our objective should be to use our resources to carry out that vision. We believe that most people do not maximize their calling and purpose in life because they are in financial prison and constantly in a state of survival.

This book will unlock for you the steps to take to manage the resources God has given you to be financially free. You will pick up tools to maximize the active income you make currently to save as much as possible. This framework will give you understanding of who you are as an investor and how to see your strengths in light of the various passive income strategies that exist so you steward those resources as well.

Why is all of this so important? Because once you obtain Financial Freedom you will continue in service to others. You were never meant to "retire." That word means to be taken out of service.

You were meant to wisely manage what God has given you in order to be a blessing to others. So with this in mind, we invite you into this exciting process of discovering who you are and how you can be free to reflect your creator in the way you were meant to.

This is the abundant life!

INTRODUCTION

"And let us not grow weary of doing good, for in due season we will reap, if we do not give up."

—GALATIANS 6:9

At the time this book is written, as the words run through the printing press, the binding holds the pages together, and our smiling faces sit on the back cover, there is $6.7 trillion stored in 401(k) plans in America. In a previous life, before the two of us would create this community that has come to be Wealth Without Wall Street, this statistic might have stuck out to us as a positive—*Oh wow, this means there are a lot of people well on their way to a comfortable retirement.*

But that was back before our eyes were opened to the abundance of opportunities out there. More importantly, this was before we were truly aware of what it meant to be financially free. It was back before Wealth Without Wall Street, when our only interactions with each other occurred as members of the local church. It was back in the early 2000s, years before one particular book exchange would take us on a journey more important than any we had been on before.

Back in those early days when our hair was a little thicker and our waistlines were a little thinner, we held different occupations: Joey was a mortgage loan officer and Russ a Certified Financial Planner.

For Russ, being in the finance business meant spending his days giving clients advice on investment strategies. His training taught him to help people create wealth through retirement plans that ran through Wall Street. For years, that was what happened. It's how his training taught him to think: to believe that retirement plans were built on mutual funds, exchange-traded funds (ETFs), and other advertised paths.

For Joey, being in the mortgage industry meant being heavily dependent on referrals to build a client list. So having a friend whose clients were always looking to grow their net worth was a good thing, because real estate has been a top choice of wealth-building for years. And who better than that good friend to gain him some referrals?

It took much longer than Joey had hoped to get Russ to send over some referrals, but in the end, he finally did. Why the long wait? That will soon become clear.

Sometime around 2010, Russ finally agreed to send some referrals Joey's way. But it came at a cost. "I'm not going to refer any clients to you," Russ said, "until you read this book. Because without this book you won't understand the strategies I'm teaching my clients." That book was *Becoming Your Own Banker* by R. Nelson Nash. It was a book that would change the course of both of our lives.

"No problem," Joey said.

Russ's response caught Joey a little off guard. "That'll be twenty bucks, by the way."

Yes, Russ charged for the book exchange. Some friendship, isn't it?

The book that exchanged hands that day is still just as insightful and relevant now as it was when it was written. It discusses the Infinite Banking Concept™ (IBC), which offers an unconventional path to Financial Freedom. The IBC idea was first planted into Russ's mind during a conference he attended in January 2009—during the depths of the financial collapse when the housing market, the stock market, and many other common investment paths were taking a beating. He and, to his surprise, only about three hundred other finance professionals and certified public accountants (CPAs) attended the conference to learn about this little-known strategy.

Why isn't anyone else doing this? Russ thought to himself as he sat in the half-empty room. Infinite Banking seemed to be an answer to everyone's concern for financial security and freedom—the hidden gem no one else knew about. From then on, Russ changed his entire strategy for his clients. He opened their eyes to the truth about Wall Street, and he hasn't looked back since.

For Joey, those twenty dollars he handed over for the book may have been the best he ever spent. At the time he read it, he was already making good money—more than $300,000 a year—as a mortgage loan officer, but he didn't realize how much he was leaving on the table. Raising a family with young kids, he was preparing himself for a lot of responsibility. He needed to ensure he had money put away for the near future and was weighing his options for college savings. He was contemplating the 529 college savings plan and trying to decide which retirement plan would suit him best—both Wall Street paths—when *Becoming Your Own Banker* landed in his hands.

The Infinite Banking Concept came to us both at the perfect time.

Infinite Banking created such clarity for the two of us that we decided it was necessary to keep digging. We researched, we found new and unique strategies—both inside IBC and out—and used this knowledge to create passive income that continues to grow.

The information continued pouring in, so much so that in 2014, the full-time jobs we once held were a thing of the past. We partnered together and went on a mission of lifelong learning. And, more importantly, of sharing what we learned. Just two short years later, we started the Wealth Without Wall Street movement. Knowing we were on to something, we wanted to share our knowledge with as many other folks as we could. Since then, we have continued to seek unique ways to make money without having it tied up in Wall Street. Through our online community, our podcast, and now through this book, we continue to help share this knowledge.

THE THREE-STEP PROCESS TO FINANCIAL FREEDOM

Both of us had life-changing experiences when we discovered alternate paths to investing that we hadn't known about before. We had both been convinced over the years—as has most of the country—that the paths available through Wall Street were the only options for investing and retirement savings. Yet as we navigated away from the common investment routes and did more research into Wall Street's alternatives, we became more confident in our abilities to create our own wealth. As time went on, our schedules began to open up. We had more time to spend with our families, more money to provide them with a comfortable lifestyle, and more energy to dive into new and exciting investment opportunities.

As we continued to dive into these exciting paths that offered us financial security, we also uncovered the lies of Wall Street and learned why they are so determined to get their hands on our money. For example, the word "retirement" *only* benefits Wall Street. It's a scare tactic—a way to get you to give them your cash so that they can use it to make *themselves* money. *You* take the risk by placing your money into the market and others make money off of that risk, yet the payout for you is often minimal.

Let's put that into context to help clarify. Think about this for a second. Imagine you are about to enter into a business partnership. In this partnership, you are the one who puts up all the money, you take all the risk, yet your business partner is the one who gets to make the final decisions. This is especially true when it comes time to divide profits—your partner determines how much of a cut you get.

Sound like a good deal? Of course it doesn't, but that's the partnership nearly one-third of Americans have with the Internal Revenue Service, or the IRS, when they open retirement accounts.

When you find alternative ways of investing outside of Wall Street, you open up your mind to endless possibilities. You are no longer limited to the small window of options offered through stocks and bonds. Instead, you have the entire world in front of you. Once your eyes are opened, you can see the potential in real estate investing, in IBC, land-flipping, lending, and so much more.

Look at the two of us, for example. We're two guys whose eyes have been opened to the possibilities and now we have more LLCs between the two of us than we do kids—and combined, we have nine kids.

This book is a culmination of everything we have learned

since the day Nelson Nash's incredible book exchanged hands. We have taken all of our research and all of our trials—including all of our errors—and devised a plan that has proven to be valuable, both to our clients and to ourselves. We have taken all of this planning and put everything together into a simple, three-step process:

GOAL

Many people aren't sure what they want. They hear fearful statistics about retiring and tell themselves that they're missing out if they don't start accounts through their job or invest in some sort of individual retirement account (IRA) or 401(k). But they have no other plans for their future, which means they won't know how much money they'll need. They simply make decisions based on fear of the unknown. In Step One, a person must identify their wants, needs, and their overall Goal.

PLAN

Once a decision is made *to* start investing, the new investor will typically hand money over to mutual funds or another "easy button" investment path. Doing so will make a person think they're making a good decision by investing, but they have no idea what happens with their money after they hand it over. Essentially, they are handing over control. In Step Two, one must create a roadmap for what they want and where they want to be in life. At what age would you like to be financially free? How does your Investor DNA align with the investment paths you are looking to pursue? Building out a step-by-step Plan allows one to accomplish their Goal.

SUPPORT

As one ventures down this new path they have discovered, they will need some Support. They will want help and guidance along the way and since many of our friends, family, and colleagues still follow the path of 401(k) and IRA Plans, that Support might not be readily available. By joining a community of like-minded individuals and having professional Support on hand, mistakes can be avoided and Goals and Plans can become more likely to be achievable in a shorter period of time.

Goal, Plan, Support—this is your **GPS** navigation system that will take you from where you are today to where you want to be later in life. It will be your navigational beacon toward Financial Freedom.

Since 2016, we have been researching new and unique methods of obtaining passive income so that we can have Financial Freedom today, rather than waiting until what Wall Street calls a "retirement age." As we continue to learn and expand our strategies, we have been sharing our results with the Wealth Without Wall Street community in hopes it drives others to create their own Goals and Plans. Along the way, we have created a Support system for those who desire expert guidance or to simply interact with other individuals on the same path.

With this book, we're casting a wider net to share our knowledge with you. We know it's hard to make the leap from the "safe" investments of Wall Street. But once you understand the lies Wall Street tells and realize the consistency and potential of alternative investments, you'll no longer fear exchanging Wall Street for something new. So we want to help you create your own Goals and your own Plan. We explain how your actions can allow you to create your own mailbox money lifestyle, where passive income rolls in without trading your time in exchange.

That being said, we do have to get a little disclaimer out of the way. The information contained within this book isn't meant to be advice. It's not a written Plan for you to follow. What we're doing is simply sharing what we have found to be successful and hoping it provides some insight into what you can do to move yourself closer to your own Financial Freedom. Nothing will happen overnight, but we hope that what you retain here will help guide you toward a path much better aligned with your future Goals.

REMEMBER, THIS IS A PROCESS

Our three-step process was designed over the course of many years working together. It wasn't something we threw together overnight and started sharing with the world. It took time for us to perfect this process and the guidelines within. And it will take you time to perfect this process as well.

This book isn't a get-rich-quick scheme. There are too many of them out there and we're not here to collect your money and run away with it. After all, that's what Wall Street does and we're not part of it. Here, some thinking will be required, as will a bit of legwork.

If you're patient, this process will work for you. But there will be work to put in beforehand. As the famous saying goes, *nothing good comes easy*. You may need to have a five-to-nine after your nine-to-five ends for a few years but it will be worth it in the long run. If you put in the work now, the rewards will come later. You will not only improve your own financial life, but the knowledge you gain while doing so will help your children and will allow them to pass these values down to their children and so on.

Want to know the best part about this process, though? There's no experience necessary to succeed. You don't need our background in finance or years' worth of studying to succeed with this formula. All you need is an open mind and a passion to get back some of your time without suffering financially.

Remember, Wall Street is the easy button. It's designed that way to make it as effortless as possible for you to hand over your money. At the opening of this introduction, we mentioned that $6.7 trillion is locked up in retirement accounts, and that comes out of the pockets of the nearly 100 million Americans who participate in these Plans. These are the sort of numbers Wall Street needs to continue raking in their own piles of cash that *your* money creates. And they have creative ways of ensuring you continue to contribute, like taking "pretax money," which really just allows them to take your money before you even get a chance to see it.

The worst part of all is that your money is tied up, unable to be accessed without a penalty until you are 59 ½ years old. Do you really want to wait that long? Will your spouse and kids want to wait that long for you to stop working long hours (those hours you need to keep working just to be able to continue investing into that fund)?

Think of it this way. Will your daughter want you to push her on the swings when you're sixty and she's in her thirties? Will your son want you to build Legos with him or throw a baseball in the yard when he's pushing forty and you finally have some free time on your hands?

What you're giving up by trading your time for money right now are these things that you will never be able to get back. It's about time—preserving time and being able to spend it with your family, or doing things that you want to be doing. Your children will never be the same age again. They will never be the age that they are *right now* ever again. *You* will never be this age again.

Our mission through this book and through our Wealth Without Wall Street community is to give you time back *now*. Today. So that you can enjoy your life now rather than defer until you hit a "retirement age."

Are you ready to take the next step toward gaining Financial Freedom and opening up endless opportunities to create cash flow? Join us as we walk you through this process. Let's begin with Step One: Creating your crystal-clear Goal.

STEP ONE

A CRYSTAL-CLEAR GOAL

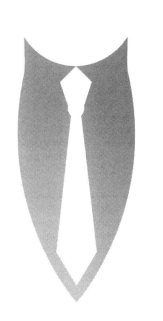

CHAPTER ONE

WHAT IS FINANCIAL FREEDOM TO YOU?

"For you were called to freedom, brothers. Only do not use your freedom as an opportunity for the flesh, but through love serve one another."

—GALATIANS 5:13

If money wasn't an obstacle, how would your life look?

It's an age-old question. One that each of us has heard at least once in our lifetime. It brings visions of yachts, jets, beaches, and relaxation—the celebrity lifestyle that's put on display for the world to salivate over.

But is that really what everyone would be doing if there was no need to worry about money? Is that what *you* would be doing? Would you be cruising on a yacht or lying on a beach every single day for your entire life?

Your immediate response might be *yes* with a big grin on your face, thinking about the relaxation and the luxury. But is that really what you would be doing? Wouldn't that get a little bit boring after a while? Wouldn't you want to get up and go do something?

Of course. We all would. We all strive for greatness in some fashion. Whether it be spending time with our families, starting businesses that can change the world, or developing relationships we wouldn't have had time to do in the past, we all want more. Each of us has a vision of what a better life would look like yet our need to produce an income usually gets in the way of those Goals. We have no free time.

That was the reason Joey left his $300,000 a year job as a mortgage broker to be part of the Wealth Without Wall Street movement. It was because he was tired of being married to his work phone. Sure, he made great money and could afford to take his family on vacations, but what fun was a vacation when his cell phone was mounted to his hip and he wasn't able to spend quality time with his wife and children?

Neither of us enjoyed the life of being away from our families. We wanted to spend more time with them without having to sacrifice our income. That was our idea of a dream life.

On the other hand, *our* version of life unbound by finances may not be appealing to others. People who are in life scenarios different from ours won't want the same things. They may want that yacht or that lifelong beach vacation. And there's nothing wrong with that. Because to them, *that's* freedom.

The term *Financial Freedom* has been gaining a lot of popularity recently. Seeing several incredible economic collapses in the matter of two decades will certainly have that effect on a population. People want to ensure their financial security. They want to make sure their families and loved ones are protected from another catastrophic event, so they have taken an interest in studying personal finance habits.

At Wealth Without Wall Street, we're no different. Our

number one Goal is to ensure that everyone in our community is prepared for the unknowns that may arise—to ensure the safety and well-being of everyone and their families.

However, for us, the term Financial Freedom is approached from a different angle. Rather than asking the question of *What do you need to be financially free?*, we ask, *What is Financial Freedom to you?* Because different people want different things. They have different Goals in life. Have different opinions on what freedom really is.

This is why we've found Step One to be the most critical starting point for anyone venturing out into the world of personal finance:

Goal.

You need a clearly defined Goal. Before stepping into the vast world and figuring out how to attain Financial Freedom, you first need to know what you determine *is* freedom to you.

Where are you in life? Where do you want to be? How do you want to spend your time? What do you need to do now, today, to ensure that you are able to start spending your time the way you want to spend it and not how you *think* you need to spend it?

In order to have clarity in your path to Financial Freedom, you need to define that overall Goal. To do that, we need to talk about the stereotypes associated with money and this new idea of Financial Freedom.

THE IDEA AS A WHOLE

What is your calling? What are you meant to do in this world? We all have something we're so extremely passionate about that we think about it night and day, don't we? Now, what if you could put all of your energy into pursuing that passion instead of wasting precious time doing something you don't love so that you can pay the bills?

The idea of freedom has always been there. Each of us seeks it. It's why we look forward to the weekends and vacations. We want an escape. But what if your entire life could be an escape? Seem impossible? We assure you, it isn't.

This whole idea of opening up more time for yourself is becoming increasingly more popular. *FIRE* is what a lot of people are calling this Financial Freedom movement, and it stands for *Financial Independence, Retire Early*. The movement is filled with people whose hope is to save large portions of their income so that they can exit the workforce early.

While we don't necessarily have anything against retiring early from a job you may not love, it's that word *retire* that we take offense to. Our calling—our reason for being put on this earth—is to produce. By taking oneself out of the workforce, or retiring, a mindset shift occurs that makes someone believe that they have reached their Goal. But we believe that the Goal should be to move into something more productive—something that aligns more with one's beliefs and values—rather than a state of doing nothing.

For the two of us, the Goal has been to spend time with our families while also making money. It's something we both loved doing, going back to when we were simply church friends who lived separate professional careers. It's what we have wanted for so long and we were lucky enough to find a way to do it. We determined our Goal and we pursued it.

Most working Americans have been led to believe that the only path to Financial Freedom is through the stock market. They have taken the bait of promises to have over several million dollars sitting in an account one day. But is Financial Freedom really about deferring life for forty or fifty years? Is it about throwing a chunk of every paycheck toward a prayer, that the stock market will continually rise during the decades you are contributing to it?

Let's make one thing clear, though: reaching for this easy-button solution isn't the fault of the contributor. If you have a 401(k), an IRA, or some other retirement account on Wall Street, you haven't made any wrong decisions. What's happened is that you have been marketed to by companies with large pockets and large advertising budgets.

Wall Street needs your money, plain and simple. In fact, they need the money so badly that they're willing to set up these retirement plans with your employers so that they can get your money *before you even have a chance to see it*. And if you consider that most financial advisors are taught in their training to sell mutual funds for these mutual fund companies, it makes it even easier to believe that there is little to no focus on actual wealth building.

This strategy is nothing new. From experience, we know this to be true. It's why Russ has voluntarily stripped the CFP® (CERTIFIED FINANCIAL PLANNER™) from his title. It's because the industry was exposed, and once this concept revealed itself, it became clear it wasn't a desired path to continue down.

We like to focus on a better solution. One that allows us to use our money to invest in things that can generate cash flow *today*, not forty or fifty years from now. We like to invest in assets that produce *passive income*, not in ventures that we hope will appreciate and accumulate a large pot of gold one day.

We like to shove aside the easy button we've been advertised and opt instead into something a little more fun and, more importantly, that we have control over. We want control and we want to see returns on our investments today. That's why we chase after passive income instead of locking away our funds in a Wall Street vault. We pursue cash flow that we can see—a tangible result of our investing efforts.

What is *passive income*? It's income you make while you sleep. Money that continues to pour in whether you are around or not. It's the opposite of *active income*, which is the income you trade your time for—that hourly wage or annual salary that requires you to sacrifice your time in exchange for that paycheck.

And what is cash flow? Cash flow is the monthly revenue you make from those *passive income* streams. It is what gives you the ability to have freedom by being able to cover your monthly expenses. This is one of the most important topics we highlight here at Wealth Without Wall Street, and it's displayed in such a simple formula:

PI > ME

When your passive income is greater than your monthly expenses, you are financially free.

The formula may seem simple—and for the most part, it is—but getting that passive income side to be greater than the monthly expenses side is certainly no easy task. It takes time and dedication, but with a clearly defined Goal in place, it becomes much more certain that you can attain this reality.

With this simple little formula now in place, you can pull the curtain back and see all the other options available to you that you couldn't see before. Investment opportunities open up. You no longer view your investments as limited. You can review all these new options and evaluate each to see which are best suited for you (more on Investor DNA in Chapter Eight) and can invest in the paths that interest you the most.

FREEDOM

Forget about what everyone else is doing for a second. Focus instead on what you want. Focus on what it is you think would create more freedom in your life. Think about your own version of Financial Freedom and then ask yourself this very simple question:

Is what I'm doing today getting me closer to my Goals or farther away? The answer to this question will provide a crystal-clear vision of where you are and where you want to be.

Joey found himself asking this question back when he was working for a Fortune 50 company, reeling in a high salary but sacrificing so much in the process. A real game-changer occurred during an event many of you can certainly relate to.

Picture yourself driving your young daughter to school. It's rare that you're home enough to be able to take her and you revel in the moment, looking back at her as she's all bundled up in her big coat and scarf, looking out the window. She's young and energetic so the silent ride doesn't last long. She asks, "Are you going to pick me up today after school?"

"I can't today, honey," you say through a smile.

She moves her gaze from the window to the rearview mirror where she can see you. "Why not?"

"Well, because I have to work," you try to explain. "And I'll still be working when you get done with school."

"But why do you have to work?"

"Because I need to pay the bills, sweetie."

"Why do you have to pay the bills?"

"Well, because I need to pay for this car that we're driving. You want me to have this car, don't you?"

"Yes."

"And you want us to have our house, right?"

"Yes."

"Well I need to work so that I can have the money to pay for those things."

"But I don't get it. We already *have* a car. And we already *have* our house. So you can stop going to work."

It would be great if life worked that way, wouldn't it? But as adults, we know that's not the truth. Joey found this to be true from the exact example above, because this same scenario took place one morning as he took one of his daughters to school.

It was an innocent conversation but one that made him realize that he had to go to work because work was his only source of a paycheck. He really had no passive income at the time and this conversation became the motivator in his mind to push him to create more passive income—enough so that he would never again have to tell his daughter that he had to work when she wanted him to be there to pick her up from school.

We know that we cannot pay off an entire lifestyle—that we will always need to have a steady flow of income if we want to be financially free. It's inevitable that we will need to spend some time away from our families, working, but we don't have to be absent so often. We *do* have options.

In our Inner Circle—an integral part of our Wealth Without Wall Street community—we get all sorts of responses as to why people want to be financially free: people who join this group by saying they want to spend more time with their family, they want to be able to serve others or pursue some adventure they've always wanted to pursue but can't do while locked into a job.

The answers vary widely, and it's pretty interesting to say the least. What it shows, though, is that we all have a different idea of what freedom actually is. Each of us has this vision of a great life that we could have if we weren't burdened by the things we need to do to pay those bills.

What we teach in our Inner Circle is that this idea of Financial Freedom doesn't have to be a fantasy. It can be a reality. You just have to have a clearly defined Goal. You have to know what it is you want to achieve and then make a Plan toward pursuing that vision. And there is one important concept we teach that can really open your mind to answer these questions: *Time, Treasure, Tradition.*

TIME, TREASURE, TRADITION

For us, there are three things we want out of life: more time, a sense of purpose, and to hand down generational wealth to our children. Ultimately, we want to build passive income to become who God has created us to be, unhindered by finances and the stresses related. Once those things are removed, we can grow into the strengths we have and we can serve others better.

Now, everyone has a different perspective. Different people have different ideas of what they want—we've already talked about this. But for the most part, broadly speaking, these are the three desirables of anyone seeking a better life.

Let's walk through each of them, starting with Time.

Time

Is it not the most valuable resource? In our examples to this point, have you not nodded your head at least once and thought to yourself that you don't want anything holding you back from spending time with loved ones? Or from creating memories with those closest to your heart?

If this is true, then why do we spend so much of our time on other people's schedules? Why do we let our jobs dictate how we allocate our time? Why is it that we spend so much time working for other people when, deep down, we want to be doing something else—*anything* else?

It's simple, really. It's because we *have* to pay the bills. The example above that talks about our innocent little kids asking why we have to go to work is a prime example of why we do what we do.

But do we have to? Is being an employee our only option? Must we sacrifice every weekday of our lives just so we can have the things that we want? Isn't there a way that we can buy back some of that time so that we can enjoy it doing what we want to do?

Of course there is. And it may seem like such a simple concept to think about, but the first step to taking back some of that precious time is to know that you *do* have other options.

Treasure

Wealth isn't simply about taking your time back, but about enjoying that free time by living your life to the fullest. It's about being able to bring things into your life that you never could before. Instead of having to cram all the kids into your little sedan, you can now afford to go out and buy that SUV without grinding your teeth at night worrying about how you're going to pay for it. And if your house seems too small for that growing family of yours or you wish you lived in an area with better public schools, you can now more seriously consider moving into that dream home of yours.

Treasure goes further than purchases that will make your everyday life easier. You can also start looking into the treasures you never dreamed of having. That lake house? You can have it now. No longer do you need to scroll through Airbnb listings with your spouse for weeks on end to see what's in your budget. Having Financial Freedom gives you the chance to *own* that lake house. And look at that, you open up more time in your life by not having to search for the next family vacation destination—you already have the perfect place.

If you're thinking to yourself, *Russ and Joey, why in the world would I buy a lake house and take on that added expense if I'll only be there a few weeks out of the year?!* Well then, you'll really enjoy some of the content we have put together in Chapters Nine and Ten. Particularly, the discussion on short-term rentals. Because that lake house you just bought? It doesn't have to be an expense; it can be an asset that generates additional passive income.

Dream a little bit here. Think about some of the things that would seriously simplify your life. Go through your typical day and pick out the things that bring you stress. Now imagine the tangible treasures that can make all that stress go away. Believe it or not, these things can be within reach.

Tradition

Are you excited about the idea of attaining wealth? Find yourself all fired up about the possibility of enhancing your lifestyle? We're both right there with you. Remember, we had occupations that earned us a good income before we decided to go on this adventure, but we still weren't satisfied. We still didn't feel that sense of fulfillment.

We also have the same concerns over our kids' futures as you do. We want the absolute best for our children. We don't want to see them repeat the same issues and struggle financially into their adult years.

Tradition is about creating something that lasts longer than we will, or longer than our children will, for that matter. It is about creating a legacy that starts with us and then is passed down through generations. Tradition is a legacy of learning and teaching that can be handed down so that the true value of building wealth continues without us.

By providing our children with the proper guidance, we create the opportunity for them to teach these concepts to their children, and so on and so on until all the Morgans and the Murés and every child with your last name is able to live a life where time can remain their number one asset.

There needs to be an apprentice process within a family, or a way to make sure all family members are on the same page as it relates to how to generate income, how to handle money, and how to be charitable.

FINANCIAL FREEDOM STARTS WITH ACCESSIBILITY

What are we consistently taught about attaining wealth? What does every financial guru tell us is the path we should take?

It's those paths that work as an extended savings Plan, right? The ones that put our money away in some untouchable place. *It's for your own good*, we're told. *Untouchable means that it is bound to grow without interference.*

It's a good story to tell. It resonates with the average person who feels as though they would be tempted to tap into that money. This sales pitch also reassures people that they won't have to work forever, and that they will have enough money to live comfortably during the years they're no longer in the work force.

Compounding your money is great; we won't deny that. But what if we could compound money on our own? What if we could access our money today and use that money to have unlimited growth? Wouldn't it be better if we could use our money to do the things we enjoyed best, opening up the opportunity for more Time, Treasure, and Tradition?

Financial freedom doesn't come from setting aside 20 percent of your income for decades. Think about that. Think about what you're being told: hand over a large fraction of your income every week and we'll allow you to have it back in a few decades.

The first thing that comes to mind is your income today. How many people struggle to pay their bills as it is? There are a lot of people living paycheck to paycheck, and by not having access to all of their funds, they are limiting themselves to what they are able to enjoy at this point in their lives. But, again, we're sold on this idea of more money in the future.

Wall Street wants to hold onto your money. A 401(k), IRA, 529 college savings Plan—these all make your money inaccessible for long periods of time, meaning you can't use it to create cash-flowing passive income that you can see *today*. But what's more important than that is the fact that Wall Street holding onto your money and promising you returns in a few decades means you aren't thinking. Giving your money to these "gurus" means that your money is out of sight, out of mind. You then avoid the responsibility of having to do anything with it.

Why in the world would you want to do that? This is *your* future that's being built here, not somebody else's. Everything should revolve around what *you* want and what *you* believe is best, not somebody on Wall Street whom you have never met before.

Successful people—and we're talking in terms of monetary success—always have access to their money. They use income to put toward passive income streams, then take that passive income to put into even more passive income streams. They have an Action Plan for every move they make and they can only have this Action Plan because they have access to their money.

WHAT'S YOUR ACTION PLAN?

Knowing what you want is the first step to gaining clarity with your situation—toward achieving your Goal. But having actionable steps toward achieving that Plan is just as important as having one Plan. Because an Action Plan is only that: a Plan. It doesn't do you any good to have a Plan if you aren't going to act on it or follow through with it.

You must be an active participant in this Plan in order for it to come to fruition. If you wish to pursue that end Goal of Financial Freedom and the ability to open up more time in your life to do the things you're passionate about, you need to actively work for it. You need to be the one taking control and making things happen. You can do this. You can buy back your time and become who you were meant to be.

In the next chapter, we'll introduce the Financial Passport that can act as your vision board. It can be your constant reminder that the things you wish to have in life are attainable. If you continue to educate yourself on the unique ways to create passive income and stick with the Action Plan that you put in place, your life can completely transform.

What do you think, are you ready to break the stereotype of Financial Freedom only being available at retirement? Want to steer away from the financial diet we've been fed for so long that tells us the only way to a better life is to work longer hours and spend less money? What the two of us have learned over the years is that there are plenty of options to create passive income that allow you to enjoy your life *today*.

So let's get started. Begin thinking about how you can

create a Plan that consists of the most basic element of personal finance: **PI > ME**. We'll show you how to build out the rest, starting with the most basic fundamental:

To change the way you think about money.

CHAPTER TWO

CHANGE THE WAY YOU THINK

"Do not be conformed to this world, but be transformed by the renewal of your mind."

—ROMANS 12:2

What does your ideal lifestyle look like?

Before we go on and start telling you about what most people respond with during our group training and coaching sessions, think about how *you* would answer this question. How would you envision your ideal lifestyle? What would you be doing? Where would you be? Who would be there with you?

Most of us allow our imagination to take us to some tropical destination, don't we? Or to some secluded place where all the noise and stress just disappears. Is that you? Are you on an island somewhere? Alone in a house in the mountains? Taking the boat out on the lake?

If so, you're not alone. Because most people want to simply relax. They want to enjoy their time off from work and look forward to freeing their mind and doing the more enjoyable things in life.

But why is that? Why does the idea of work bring such a negative context to mind? Is it possible that people want to relax because they associate work with something that lacks passion and fulfillment? Do they view work as some sort of burden on their time, pulling them away from the things they really enjoy doing? Think about how many people in your life you have heard talk about work in a negative light. You don't have to share. We'll leave you to dwell on that a bit.

Alright, now let's try something else. We want you to keep that visual. Continue to envision your ideal lifestyle. But now, imagine those events replaying over and over again. Take the boating story, for instance. Imagine yourself taking the boat out into the water every day. Every. Single. Day. Doesn't sound so amazing now, does it? Now it just seems daunting.

You mean to tell me I have to hook this boat trailer up to the truck, drive it down to the lake, back it into the water, and drop it in, every single day? You mean I need to gas this thing up every day? Pack up a cooler with drinks and snacks every day? And then clean the boat and pull it back onto the trailer when we're done every day?

That's certainly not an ideal lifestyle, now is it? But it *is* ideal. To take the boat out for an afternoon on the lake *is* a great time, but it's not an ideal *lifestyle*—it's an ideal *day*.

An ideal lifestyle is different. It's how you will live your life for weeks, months, or years at a time. It's what gives you a reason to wake up in the morning. It's what gives you a sense of purpose. Your ideal lifestyle is one that brings the productivity you seek into your life.

So when somebody asks you now about your ideal lifestyle, remember that your ideal day is not what you want your ideal lifestyle to look like. You need to map out what you want your everyday scenario to look like and you can do so by putting together a tool that we have created for doing just that: a Financial Passport.

CREATING A FINANCIAL PASSPORT

"Paper is to write things down that we need to remember. Our brains are used to think." That quote comes from some guy named Albert Einstein. He was just somebody who still, nearly a century after his death, is considered to be the genius of all geniuses.

I don't know about you, but we like to take the advice of those who have come before us and succeeded. And if the advice comes from Albert Einstein himself? Well, that's a no-brainer—pun intended.

So the two of us write things down, and we coach everyone we work with to do the same and to get things done faster and more clearly. Because writing things down allows you not only to remember, but also to visualize. To dream. To see what you want day after day and to tackle those obstacles and achieve those Goals. Visualization allows your subconscious to work for you—to act as your supercomputer.

All of this visualization and clarity comes in the form of our Financial Passports.

When I stop trading time for money I will be able to

SUPPORT MY FAMILY WITH QUALITY TIME

"BE"	"DO"	"HAVE"

Be A Saver	**Stop Doing**	**Passive Income**
$20,000	*Keeping money in business account*	*$25,000*

Our Passports consist of our Be, Do, and Have Goals. Ones we have for the future, but also ones that we have for today. Each of our Financial Passports is filled with the things we want to accomplish, regardless of how big or small they may seem. It's like a collage—pictures filling the page. Except our collages are filled with images of Goals we want to achieve.

Yours could consist of a business you want to build, a personal Goal you're striving for, or a deadline you want to hit. Its contents can be changed as your Goals change and are used to help keep you on track toward whatever it is you need to accomplish to find your own Financial Freedom.

This Financial Passport helps you to visualize what Financial Freedom looks like so that when you get there, you recognize it. It gives you something to continually strive for and helps to keep you on track when you feel like you want to give up. And giving up will become tempting. A story of our friend, Sid, described below, will show you the depth of sacrifice some people are willing to go to make Financial Freedom a reality, but it can all be worth it once you hit those Passport Goals.

Whatever it is you choose to place on this document, having a visual helps to remind you of exactly what it is you're going after. So it should be somewhere that guarantees you see it every day. For us, that happens to be on our computer monitors. Our desktop wallpaper is littered with the ideas we are pursuing and the Goals we want to accomplish.

But the Financial Passport doesn't stop there. It isn't limited to our future financial Goals. It also includes things we want to make sure we save time for. Like dinner with our families, helping the kids with homework, and keeping time available for church during the weekends.

Yes, time should be kept open for those important things outside of work. And they should be just as important as the other Goals you are working toward in life. Because without your family and your beliefs, why else are you working so hard to achieve great things?

Be sure to prioritize the things on your Financial Passport—family and personal time included. Because Goals that involve Financial Freedom are what we all hope to achieve, but not if it comes at the cost of leaving our family and hobbies behind.

BE, DO, HAVE

As you have seen from the image in the previous section, there are three columns on the Financial Passport: *Be*, *Do*, and *Have*. If you're struggling to find ways to fill these columns on your Passport, here are some questions we like to ask:

Who do you want to become?

What do you need to stop doing?

What will you have when you are financially free?

Three pretty standard questions, aren't they? But they can provide some valuable answers. And in the process of doing so, they can tell a lot about who you are as a person and what you want in your life. These answers can be a guideline for you so that you can determine exactly what you need to gain Financial Freedom, because this won't be the same for everybody.

To give a better understanding of just how important these three questions are, let's look at the story of Sid Christensen, a member of our Wealth Without Wall Street community. He earns an income by operating an excavator but the job kept him away from his family a lot. And after a freak snowmobile accident left him with a broken leg, he sat on the top of a mountain waiting for a helicopter to pick him up and thought, *Now what?* He couldn't work, which meant he couldn't provide a full income for his family. What was he going to do?

He thought to himself that he had to find some way to bring in more income. And given his injury, active income wasn't going to cut it.

He didn't know it, but he was building out his Be, Do, Have. *What do you want to become?* A supportive husband and father.

Sid's only thought as he sat on the top of a snow-covered mountain waiting several hours for a helicopter was what he would do for money. How was he going to provide for his family now? He also had a passion for spending time with his children—now, while they are young—and being a part of their lives.

What do you need to stop doing? To find ways to not have to work so much and to spend more time with his family without sacrificing income.

He knew he needed to pay the bills and to provide a good life for his wife and children, but he was also torn. Growing up, his dad had always been working and didn't have much time to spend with him. He wanted the opposite. He didn't want to defer spending time with his children until they were older. He wanted it now. Sitting in the snow with a broken leg, he knew he wouldn't be running around with them anytime soon. But all the thoughts running through his head at that moment made him realize that it could be possible to make money while still having time to spend with them.

What do you want to have when you are financially free? More than anything, the freedom to choose what to do with his time.

He wanted to have what most people would say is impossible: more free time *and* more money. Mostly, he just wanted something different. He wanted what active income could never provide but what passive income had the potential to.

In your own life, as you search for what will offer you that Financial Freedom you seek, ask yourself these three questions.

The answers can be used for a variety of tactics to discover what it is you truly want in life. But they can be used to dig much deeper and to evaluate how you envision your life and your future.

Don't stop there, though. Because simply knowing what you want isn't going to get you from A to B. You won't attain Financial Freedom by simply answering these questions. You need to formulate a Plan to achieve your end Goal. And then, more importantly, you need to follow that Plan.

TIME MANAGEMENT

The overall Goal here is to open up more time in our lives, right? Whether or not we place reminders on our Financial Passport to spend time doing the things we love, the end result is that we are striving toward a Goal that allows us to allocate our time in any way we want.

The two of us had a conversation with a real estate investor after creating Wealth Without Wall Street, and what this man said to us was something we had completely overlooked for so long. Our Goal through this business had always been to help people open up time in their lives, and after we had a discussion with this investor, he asked a question that sort of stumped us.

"Let me ask you something," he said. "Do you track or report your time?"

Do we report our time? Like, how much time we open up in our schedules? "Well, no," we said. At the time, we didn't. We were a little too focused on *how* to open time and less focused on the amount of time we were opening.

"Isn't time the most important thing?" the man asked.

It is. And from that conversation, the two of us looked at each other and realized that we needed to add a new metric to our system. An important metric at that. Before this conversation, we knew that freeing up time was our Goal, but we didn't emphasize the importance of managing that free time.

Why is it so important? That's because it can be so easy for each of us to do all this work, put processes in place that open up time for us, and then go fill that free time with things that fall outside of our Goals. For example, if your Goal is to spend more time with your family and you are able to accomplish this Goal by setting up passive income streams, then you have taken the first step toward accomplishing your mission. But, if you end up filling that void in time with something not in line with your Goals, then you haven't managed your time properly.

It's easy to lose focus on how important time is as we go on this journey to create financial independence. We can become so consumed with what we're doing that we forget what it was we sought out in the first place. Plus, life moves fast. New ideas can pop up at any moment. It's easy to get lured into new, time-consuming opportunities.

This is another area where writing things down can help to clarify your Goals. What the two of us do, and what we have taught others in our community to do as well, is to create a Time Awareness Log—something that was created after we had that eye-opening conversation with the real estate investor.

The idea is simple: Write down your daily activities in a time log. How do these activities match with what your future plans are for your time? Are the things you're doing wasteful or are they focus-oriented? Are they aligned with what you want to be doing or are the things you spend time on the last tasks in the world you want to be taking on?

Tracking your time and activity allows you to focus on what you do throughout the day and also tells you whether or not it's moving you forward in life. And here's a Pro Tip—something we have done in the past and has been helpful in driving us closer to our goals:

Fill out your *Ideal* Time Awareness Log.

This won't be one that tracks what you're currently doing. Rather, it lists how you would spend your time if you had financial freedom. By doing this, you can compare where you are side by side with your current Time Awareness Log. From there, you can make the necessary adjustments to move you in the right direction.

Tracking your time can be simple, especially if you use the Time Awareness Log we have created. You can find it at www.wealthwithoutwallstreet.com/book. Fill it out, take a picture of it, and place that picture inside your Financial Passport.

TIME AWARENESS LOG

	DATE	START TIME	END TIME	TIME ELAPSED	CATEGORY	ACTIVITY DESCRIPTION
	Example	*11:59 am*	*12:00 pm*	*0:01*	*W/D*	*Watching Netflix*
		12:00 am		0:00		
		12:00 am		0:00		
		12:00 am		0:00		
		12:00 am		0:00		
		12:00 am		0:00		
		12:00 am		0:00		
		12:00 am		0:00		
		12:00 am		0:00		
		12:00 am		0:00		
DAY 1		12:00 am		0:00		
		12:00 am		0:00		
		12:00 am		0:00		
		12:00 am		0:00		
		12:00 am		0:00		
		12:00 am		0:00		
		12:00 am		0:00		
		12:00 am		0:00		
		12:00 am		0:00		
		12:00 am		0:00		
		12:00 am		0:00		

wealthwithoutwallstreet.com/book

I bet you didn't expect to pick up a personal finance book that's geared toward tracking your time, did you? You might have expected that we would suggest you track your spending—and we will, don't worry—but not your time.

It's your time, though, that you are looking to open up, isn't it? Financial freedom is all about having the freedom to step away from the things you dislike doing. It's about being able to make decisions based on your happiness and not about what you're required to do so that you can pay the bills.

And that leads us to our next topic that's such a blur for most people—a myth that so many buy into. The false belief that a high income is the answer to one's financial struggles.

THE HIGH INCOME MYTH

Neither of us are strangers to exchanging our time for money. One of us being a former financial advisor and the other a mortgage loan originator, we know what it's like to have to sacrifice precious hours to turn a profit. Hey, if that's what we needed to do to provide for our families at the time, then so be it. And the same goes for you. Family comes first.

But we want to debunk a little myth here while we're discussing your mindset shift. And that's the myth that you need a high income to be able to achieve Financial Freedom. That's simply not true, and we know this because we have people in our community who are teachers, firefighters, and others who hold positions that don't pay six figures, yet they have achieved Financial Freedom.

Earning a higher income is never a bad thing. Bringing more money in the door is never going to be a negative. However, if you don't earn a ton of money, that doesn't mean you cannot pursue this idea of Financial Freedom. It doesn't mean you are doomed to spend your time working in a job you dislike while others around you are building their passive income streams.

More money through your active income stream doesn't immediately guarantee you success with passive income, or any investment strategy. Again, it doesn't hurt. But if you have ever played the Cashflow board game (a game we highly recommend), you would know that being a janitor doesn't automatically mean the game is over for you, or that being a doctor doesn't bring you into the winner's circle. Someone with either of these occupations can achieve Financial Freedom. It just depends on what they do with the money they earn.

EXPENSES

A higher income can also lead some people toward higher expenses. It's because your expenses grow proportionate to your income. The more we make, the more we end up spending.

That being said, just because you *can* doesn't mean you *should*. When it comes to expenses, we all have the ability to fall into this trap that makes us think we can safely increase our spending once more money starts to come in. It's so easy to start adding that monthly passive income to our active income and planning our expenses based on the two combined.

But remember the magic formula: **PI > ME**. If passive income is greater than monthly expenses, you're fine. However, when you start adding that active income on top, you get yourself in trouble. Because that active income might not be steady or guaranteed.

We all work hard so that we can have finer things in life, right? And that's perfectly fine. If you want that nice, new car, go out and get it. If you want a bigger house for your family or you want to travel more often, those are great things to work hard for. Your family will deserve those things, too, if they had to put up with your financial hardships as you took risks to grow your income streams.

All we're saying is that you should buy these things with money generated from income-producing assets. If you have money, first put it into an asset that generates monthly passive income for you. Then use that monthly passive income to start making purchases that will add to your monthly expenses.

Also, remember one very important concept: *a luxury once enjoyed becomes a necessity once you get a taste for it*—a phrase Nelson Nash would say all the time. Be careful of your spending habits because, remember, the end Goal here is to open up more time in your life, not to continue pushing the boundaries of your spending.

QUIT THINKING FINANCIAL FREEDOM IS FOR RETIREMENT

Russ and Joey, what's going on here? I thought this book was about personal finance and how you can help me make more money. Why are we talking about salaries and expenses? Am I missing something?

That's the best part. It *is* about making more money. But there are foundational principles we need to take care of first. Things that you can do to alter the course of your future before even making a single investment decision. All you need to do is change the way you view your financial situation. Change the way you think.

There is a lot of misinformation surrounding Financial Freedom. Most associate it with retirement and investing a certain percentage of your income every year that you can finally tap into when you're in your midsixties. The first thing we tell any of our clients, our community members, our friends, family, colleagues, and whoever else we come across is that this way of thinking has to be challenged in your mind.

This is the way Wall Street wants you to think because they want you to believe they are your only option. They do this so that they can get their hands on your money and keep it for a long time, earning *them* more money over time. They paint this illusion that the only way to accumulate wealth is to do so for an extended period of time through them.

That's not true at all.

Let's get rid of this ridiculous mindset that the only way to live a stress-free life is to defer everything until some fictional date. Financial freedom is attainable *today*. But the only way to start living the life you want is to get started.

By having a clearly defined Goal and changing the way you think, you have already opened up the possibility of a better life.

Ready to create your own Financial Passport and start improving your life today? Visit www.wealthwithout wallstreet.com/book to start your own Financial Passport.

CHAPTER THREE

KNOW YOUR GOALS

"The plans of the diligent lead to profit, as surely as haste leads to poverty."
—PROVERBS 21:5

Opening up your mind to new ways of thinking is one way to gain clarity, but knowing your Goals enables you to map out your next steps forward. Without clear Goals, your vision becomes blurred. Or, in one example, ends up with some light fixtures ending up in the craziest of places.

Check out these pictures.

One of us—one would say the *better looking of the two* but the other doesn't necessarily agree—had a custom home built a few years back. It was Russ and his wife's first time being able to have a home custom-designed and -built. The process was supposed to be exciting, but it turned out to be anything but. It was actually a little overwhelming.

There's a lot that goes into building a home, and as someone with little experience in the process, Russ made the choice to allow the builders to take control. After all, this was what they did for a living. The assumption was that they would handle the project in a professional, experienced manner—the same assumption one would have when working with any company.

Before the chaos began, everything seemed great. Research was done before Russ and his wife signed on the dotted line. The builder was referred by a trusted friend and when we met with this builder, they assured us that they had been down this road before and had everything handled.

Good, we thought. After all, we were professionals in renting property, not building it.

But the result didn't end up as promised. As you can see from the pictures, things didn't exactly line up right. The light fixture in the dining room isn't centered over where the table is supposed to go. Another fixture in the second image isn't placed between the two windows the way it should be.

And there are more issues around the house that aren't pictured here. Lights in the hallways and bedrooms weren't centered. The mirror in the bathroom wasn't centered over the faucet. In the kitchen, you couldn't have the dishwasher door open if you wanted to throw away any garbage because the cabinet door holding the trash cans and the dishwasher door would hit each other. The list goes on.

Does this scenario sound similar so far? Is it ringing any bells? Like, perhaps a typical Wall Street–based Plan—a 401(k) for example? A lack of knowledge in one area forces you to hand over control to someone else. In the case of Russ and his home, his lack of experience put them in a position where they handed over complete control to the builder. And it turned out badly.

Most people do the same thing with their finances. Since

financial education isn't taught in schools and isn't really known inside many homes, it becomes this curious topic. Much like building a home, finance is something very few people know about. The only guidance comes from friends and family members who are typically clueless themselves—no offense to those in your inner circle.

What Russ had learned through this process, and through years in the financial planning industry, is not to follow someone's verbal advice. Instead, follow what they do. If the home builder had built his own home and the sink, light fixture, and mirror didn't line up properly, would he leave it that way? Of course he wouldn't. But he was perfectly fine leaving these things in a home he wasn't living in.

The same thing can be said for receiving financial advice. Does the person giving you advice follow that advice? Do they practice what they preach or is their own investing strategy different than the one they tell you?

They wouldn't steer me in the wrong direction, right?

Of course they wouldn't. Not on purpose, at least. But if somebody is giving you financial guidance and they don't know exactly what it is that you want or need, you aren't going to end up with the result you had hoped for.

The home builders didn't misplace light fixtures, windows, cabinets, and everything else on purpose. They assumed they were doing a good job when they started putting the pieces together. They thought that their blueprints for the house were solid and that they would create a flawless dream home.

Apparently they weren't as capable as they were confident, which can be said about most of the financial advice you will hear. Friends, family, professionals—it doesn't matter. Any financial input from another person should be taken with a grain of salt.

THE PROPER GUIDANCE

By picking up this book, it's clear that you care about your finances. You want to educate yourself and form your own unique investment decisions based on your findings.

That's a great method. It's one that certainly puts you in a good place to move forward.

When it came to the house being built with so many things wrong, it grew clear that we should have taken a different path. Our proper path should have been to hire an architect to build out the design, *then* let the builder take over from there. We should have had a designer design and let the builder build.

Working with an architect would have meant getting the proper guidance. It would have meant being asked questions like, *What do you want?* and *Does this layout work for you?* Instead, all we heard was, *We'll take care of it*, and that turned out to be a bad decision.

What you can take from the home-building story is that chaos is the only thing that will come from a lack of organization and clarity. To avoid the chaos, you need to gain the proper guidance.

One of our Wealth Without Wall Street coaches is also a retired airline pilot, and one of the things he says to the clients that he speaks with is, "I can't help you pack if I don't know where you're going." It's fitting for him and something that helps him translate his message during his consultation calls.

Those consultation calls with our coaches are free, by the way, so if you're looking for that proper guidance, go to www.wealthwithoutwallstreet.com and book a free call with one of them.

But his phrase is pretty clear, and easy to translate. Nobody—not even you—can help you decide what goes into your suitcase if you don't even know where you're headed. Without a Plan in place, you're essentially flying blind. Your Action Plan is *hope*, and although hope *is* a Plan, it isn't a very reliable one.

In order to find the clarity you need to move forward with your pursuit of Financial Freedom, you need to know what you want. And that knowledge comes through education.

THE MORE YOU KNOW

Clarity never stops. It's like learning—there's always something more you can be doing to find out more. In doing so, you will continue to open your mind to new possibilities.

There's a quote from Aristotle that says, "The more you know, the more you realize you don't know." Confused? Let us write out a visual for you. One that you can do as an exercise as you read.

Draw a circle on a piece of paper. A small one, maybe the size of a bottle cap. Now look at that circle and envision that everything inside the circle is what you know. The space on the outside is information available for you to learn. But most importantly, the circle itself—the line that creates the circle—is the information that *you're aware you don't know*.

Got that? Good. Now grab something larger. Grab a coffee mug and trace the bottom of it on your paper. What do you see? A bigger circle, right? The bigger circle means that there is more space inside the circle, meaning that you have learned more.

But what about the circle itself—that line, again. Since the circle is bigger, the line that forms the circle is bigger, too. Which means that the information *we're aware we don't know* has also increased.

Everything outside the Circle is what you do not know.

The edge of what you know that you don't know.

WHAT YOU KNOW

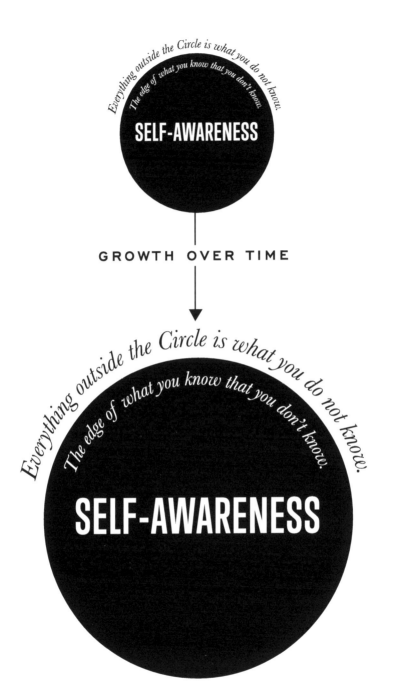

Everything outside the Circle is what you do not know.

The edge of what you know that you don't know.

SELF-AWARENESS

GROWTH OVER TIME

Everything outside the Circle is what you do not know.

The edge of what you know that you don't know.

SELF-AWARENESS

Learning is an amazing concept. It never ends. This is why nothing remains stagnant. Your job, your Plans—nothing will ever be *set it and forget it*. Neither of us stuck with the jobs we had a decade ago. We both have Financial Passports that are constantly being tweaked here and there based on the new things we consistently learn. And we are continuing to grasp the idea that there's so much more we *can* absorb.

Continuing to expand your knowledge base is important. Finding new, innovative ways to create passive income is one of the most exciting parts of our job and it's something we will continue to do. That being said, it's important not to get held back by what many people call *analysis paralysis*. This is the idea that you continue to analyze and analyze and analyze, so much that you never end up pulling the trigger on making any moves—you become paralyzed in your decision-making.

You should continually strive to improve and educate your-self on cash flow options, but not at the expense of searching for the lone, foolproof strategy. Mainly, because there is none. There are a ton of options available. And if you continue to look for that perfect Plan to place on your Financial Passport or chase after that perfect ideal lifestyle, you will never move forward.

Just as your education and knowledge expand and change, your Be, Do, Have answers may change over time. So too will your Financial Passport and one other concept we're about to introduce to you: your Financial Scorecard.

With your Financial Passport filling up and your ideal life-style mapped out, you have a pretty good visual of where you want to be. But that won't do much good if you don't know where you stand financially. Your fiscal responsibilities are equally as important.

Once you have a financial objective in place, you can start

measurably moving toward that objective. If, for example, you have a Goal to be financially free from your occupation in ten years, then you can write down the actionable steps you need to take to achieve that Goal and then begin moving forward. Using the ten-year mark, for example, you know that you need to get 10 percent closer to that Goal every year in order for it to be complete in time.

Ten years at 10 percent per year equals 100 percent.

At Wealth Without Wall Street, we created an online tool for our clients to use called the Financial Scorecard. This tool shows you how close—or far—you are from achieving your overall Goal of Financial Freedom. It not only tallies up your monthly income and expenses, but it makes calculations that help you clarify where your finances stand.

THE FINANCIAL SCORECARD

1 *Income*

2 *Fixed Expenses*

3 *Irregular Expenses*

4 *Everyday Expenses*

5 *Freedom Accounts*

6 *Balance Sheet*

INCOME *(Monthly amounts below)*

Salary

$0

Net Rental Income *(Rental Income-All Expenses)*

$0

Passive Business Income

$0

Interest/Dividents

$0

Next >

For instance, take a look at the sample Scorecard here. The top tab is the Income portion. Here, you input money coming in—your salary and any other monthly revenue you receive.

The next few tabs will consist of your various Expenses. This is the total amount of money that goes out the door every month—the total you send off to pay your bills.

Next is the Freedom Accounts portion. What are your monthly expenses for your leisure spending? What do you allocate toward this every month? You can input that number in the Freedom Accounts portion.

Finally, with your numbers put into the form, you can go to the Balance Sheet section of the card. On the top, you see Passive Income and Total Expenses with totals beneath each, pulled from the information you input to the left side of the screen.

See that small number underneath? That tells you, as a percentage, how close you are to being financially free. Because passive income—income that you generate without having to be physically present—is what will allow you to obtain that freedom. So it has to be greater than your monthly expenses because, of course, your bills still have to be paid.

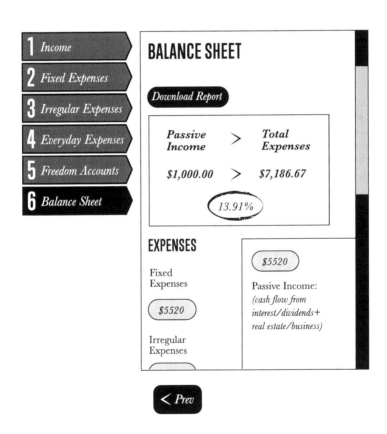

Your downloaded report also shows your Monthly Cash Flow. This takes all of your income—active income as well as passive income—and calculates it against your total monthly expenses. What remains is what you can use to invest in new opportunities such as short-term rental properties, Infinite Banking policies, land flipping, cryptocurrency mining, and many more that we will discuss in Step Two and Step Three of this book.

Think of your Scorecard as the GPS of your Action Plan. If you are about to embark on some cross-country journey, you have an idea of which direction you need to go, but without GPS coordinates pointing you to an exact location, it would be impossible to get there.

Why a GPS remark here and not a map reference? Well, for one, our kids wouldn't understand what we meant. And two, a map cannot redirect you automatically to a quicker, faster route in the middle of a drive. With the Financial Scorecard, you can have that automatic redirection when you make adjustments to your Financial Passport and incorporate them into this form.

MOVING FORWARD WITH YOUR GOAL

Once you are clear on your Goals and begin to move forward with your Financial Passport and Financial Scorecard, you move closer and closer to being independent of your salary or your full-time job. You move closer to having the time freedom you desire, and the choice to live wherever you want, travel whenever you want, and spend more time doing the things you enjoy.

Think about the added benefits of having these freedoms. Think about the stress factor alone. What would you give to be able to remove some stress from your life? Or to not have to worry about going into a job every morning that you can't stand just to work for a boss you envy? What would you give to have the ability to walk away from that job without the fear of losing your income and subsequently being cut off from being able to live your life?

There isn't enough emphasis on just how important it is to eliminate stress in your life. The chief objective of man is to glorify God and enjoy Him forever. The way we can do that is by serving others. Through doing so, we can be blessed and, in turn, continue to be a blessing to others.

God's plans weren't for you to be miserable and glide through life in misery. We're all here to do great things. The two of us have been blessed to be part of His mission to help others, and through the clarity we have gained within the financial realm, we are trying our best to do so.

With your own Goals and a clear path toward them, you, too, can make great things happen. Think about the people in your life who stand to benefit from you being a happier, healthier, wealthier person.

Don't put control of your future in the hands of a builder who has no problem leaving you with a flawed home. That's what Wall Street does with your money. They will build blindly, assuming your motivation matches theirs.

Instead, take control of your finances and build your own wealth. With your crystal-clear Goal in mind, you are already way ahead of your peers. Now it's time to take the next step, which is to design a Plan for reaching your Goal.

Want to have your own Scorecard to analyze how close you are to achieving Financial Freedom through passive income? Use the following link to get access to your own Financial Scorecard. It's free! You don't even need to join our community—although that's also free... www.wealthwithoutwallstreet.com/book.

STEP TWO

HAVE A PLAN

CHAPTER FOUR

BUDGET

"For which of you, desiring to build a tower, does not first sit down and count the cost, whether he has enough to complete it?

"Otherwise, when he has laid a foundation and is not able to finish, all who see it begin to mock him, saying, 'This man began to build and was not able to finish."

—LUKE 14:28

How much do you weigh? That's okay; you don't have to tell us. We don't really need to know; we just want to set a precedent. Because we're about to talk about the reason most people fail to hold to a budget.

What are some of the lengths you have gone to to avoid seeing the truth when stepping on the scale? Weigh yourself in the morning on an empty stomach? Step on the scale without clothes? Go for a long run beforehand?

There is a reason nobody likes to step on a scale and it's because there are few people who are happy with the result.

And the same thing can be said about one's personal finances and their budget—or lack thereof.

We don't want to see what we already know. Whether it's the scale or our personal balance sheet, most of us realize we can be doing much better at controlling the situation. And as long as we continue to trick the scale—or shove it in the closet and never pull it out to begin with—we aren't confronted with the issue.

If you want to better your finances, though, you need to pull that proverbial scale out and vow to step on it every morning. Regardless of the result, you need to be consistent with it. You need to put a Plan in place and remain consistent with that Plan. Because being consistent with it means being in control.

Did we mention being *consistent* with your Plan? There's a reason: it's because you need to remain consistent.

But there's more to a Plan than just being resolute. The problem with neglecting our weight or our spending habits is that we aren't able to take corrective actions. Instead, we avoid reality.

When we step on the scale without any tricks beforehand, the number becomes real. The same happens when we write down our numbers inside of a budget. Regardless of how bad they might be, you need to be honest with yourself—no tricks.

The unfortunate reality is that *you* were the one who made those decisions. You were the one who avoided implementing a budget. But there's a silver lining here: you have the ability to turn things around—to right the ship. You are the one in control.

AUTOMATED BUDGET

Did you fill out the Financial Scorecard using the link provided in the previous chapter? If so, it should have told you something. It should have told you if you're close to Financial Freedom or far away.

At this point in your financial journey, any number is a good number, even if it's a negative number. If your expenses are more than your income, you're in a whole world of trouble. *But*, the earlier you realize you *are* in trouble, the sooner you can begin to repair the damage using some of the tips we'll share below.

Again, any number at this point is a good number. It gives you something to work with and a goal to strive toward. With the right mindset in place and a base number to work with, you know what needs to be done. You just need some help to get there. Here are some things we've learned on our own journey to Financial Freedom.

BUDGET HACKS

You have your PI versus ME ratio in front of you. Now it's time to make some changes to open up some cash flow. Because it's this cash flow that will allow you to start expanding your investment portfolio. It will open up opportunities for you to live a better, stress-free life.

But there's more you can do. In our Automated Budgeting course, we teach some of these more detailed hacks. These are for the person who has their budget in order and is ready to take on new and exciting challenges.

PAY YOURSELF FIRST

Most people pay their bills with their paycheck. Money comes in, it's handed out to bill collectors, and then the rest is kept for investments or leisure activities. We tend to think about getting rid of those bills before we do anything else.

What if there was another way? Oh wait, there is. You can pay yourself first.

There's a book by Mike Michalowicz called *Profit First* and the central theme is to pay yourself first. That means to pay yourself before paying any of your expenses. And when it comes to investing your money, this is a critical move to ensuring that you stay on track with your future financial goals.

Paying yourself first forces you to find a way to live off of the rest. It forces you to get creative. Rather than spending freely on bills and getting creative with investments, why not spend freely on investments and find a way to get creative paying bills?

Will paying your bills get you closer to Financial Freedom? Of course not. It might keep the lights on and your family might be happy about that, but they would also be happy if you could invest more and spend less time at the office.

THE 70/30 RULE

Another common budgeting method comes from *The Richest Man in Babylon*—a highly suggested read for anyone trying to learn more about personal finance. It states a rule of investing to save 30 percent of your income and use the other 70 percent to spend.

The 70/30 rule, it's called, combined with *pay yourself first* means you put away the first 30 percent of your income for yourself. Use it toward your investments—toward reaching that overall goal on your Financial Passport. This 30 percent can be the start of your passive income streams that will gain you financial independence.

The other 70 percent is what you can use to pay your expenses. So when it comes to budgeting, be sure to only Plan on spending that 70 percent. Don't even include the other 30. Keep it set aside. Far away. Don't even be tempted to use it. You know why? Because as soon as you start tapping into that money that you should be using to *pay yourself first*, you get sucked into a bad habit that's difficult to break.

The main rule of budgeting is not to get sucked into bad habits. Once you can do this, you're well on your way to becoming a budgeting guru. And what can a budgeting guru do? They can get granular and use some of the budgeting hacks we teach to our community.

HEALTHCARE EXPENSES

It's impossible to talk about budgeting in today's world without discussing healthcare. All of life's expenses are on the rise pretty rapidly, but healthcare is one that's significantly impacting the wallets of families everywhere.

The average monthly premium for a family of four in the US is $1,152.* That's a lot of money to be dishing out each month for a little bit of coverage. And we say a little bit because a lot of those healthcare Plans have high deductibles, meaning you will be paying a lot of money out of pocket before the insurance company provides any coverage.

We manage our healthcare a bit differently. We don't have health insurance.

---

* Anna Porretta, "How Much Does Individual Health Insurance Cost," eHealth, October 1, 2022, https://www.ehealthinsurance.com/resources/individual-and-family/how-much-does-individual-health-insurance-cost.

I'm sorry, what? You two don't have health insurance?!

Yes, you heard that correctly. No health insurance for either of us or our families.

Instead, we both pay into what are called health sharing Plans. Our monthly share is around $500 per month, per family. And that covers healthcare expenses for everyone.

By doing this, we are grouping with like-minded people to share the burdens of each other—burdens greater than our ability to pay. Sound familiar? It might. This is a biblical principle from Galatians 6:2—*carry each other's burdens.*

Healthcare has become a maintenance Plan instead of insurance. That's why costs have ballooned. In our health sharing group, everyone covers the cost of their own routine doctor visits. Anything that exceeds $300 per event is then shared by everyone in the group.

For example, if one of our kids gets sick and they have to go to the doctor's office, that might cost $150 for the visit. With the health sharing Plan, we pay the entire $150 out of pocket because it doesn't hit the $300 threshold. But if something more severe were to happen and it resulted in a hospital trip that comes with a bill of say $11,000, we are only responsible for paying $300 toward the cost. The rest is covered by the shared group.

Choosing this option over health insurance not only saves us money each month inside our budget, but it gives us peace of mind that we won't get hit with a crazy, unexpected bill.

THE MORTGAGE PAYMENT MYTH

Let's start this one off with a couple of true or false questions that come from Don Blanton's software system Circle of Wealth.

A fifteen-year mortgage will save you more money over time than a thirty-year mortgage.

The interest rate is the most important factor in determining the cost of a mortgage.

A large down payment will save you more money over time than a small down payment.

Making extra principal payments saves you money.

You're more financially secure if you have your home paid off.

How many of those questions made you say *true*? How many do you think were false?

Ready for the twist? The answers are actually all the same—*they're all false*.

There is so much misinformation surrounding mortgages. People get caught up in worrying about interest rates and term lengths. Believe it or not, these are *not* the most important items to be considered. In fact, the mortgage companies *want* you to pay off the loans faster.

Why? Because they want their money back quicker so that they can use it to make more money themselves. And they also want it paid back quicker because there's less chance of you defaulting on the loan. By paying your loan back sooner, the mortgage company also beats out the rate of inflation, which causes the dollar to lose value, thus causing the mortgage company to lose money.

If the mortgage company is going through such great lengths to make their money grow as much as possible, shouldn't we be trying to do the same?

Wealth Without Wall Street isn't about taking money out of the mortgage company's pocket. We're about putting money into *your* pocket. We're in the business of helping coach our clients to create cash flow for themselves—cash flow that can be used to invest in even more revenue-generating ventures.

With that in mind, think of your mortgage in this light. Think of the monthly payment difference between a fifteen-

and a thirty-year mortgage. As an example, let's just say the monthly payment for a fifteen-year mortgage would be $2,400 and for a thirty-year mortgage, the payment is $1,800. On the surface, it might seem like paying the extra $600 is a great idea so that you can relieve yourself of a mortgage payment in half the time.

There's an opportunity cost that gets lost when you throw a higher percentage of your monthly income toward your mortgage in hopes of paying it off quicker. This eliminates the opportunity to create something that continues to pay you long after your mortgage is eventually paid off.

What could you accomplish with $108,000 ($600 per month for the next fifteen years)?

VALUE OF SAVING AN EXTRA $600 PER MONTH

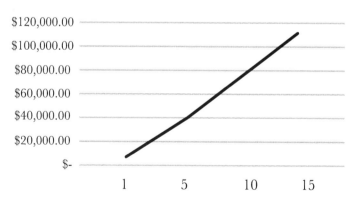

— Choosing Thirty-Year Mortgage

SEPARATING EXPENSES

We all like things to be simplified, right? And rifling through our bank statements every month to see where our money went isn't exactly the most fun thing to do. It doesn't bode well for our schedule either since it's a pretty time-consuming task.

Creating separate accounts for each of your budgeting categories simplifies things. Go back to the Financial Scorecard and look at each of the tabs. It makes sense to separate these here—wouldn't it make sense to separate them into separate bank accounts, too?

You can have separate accounts for expenses, life events, investments, and anything else you budget. You can have one that you use to save for vacations. Another to use as an emergency account. One more with money for irregular expenses.

You can even have his and hers expense accounts so that you and your significant other can have a specific budget for buying consumer goods or enjoying a relaxing night out. The options depend upon what type of expenses you have each month.

SUBSCRIPTION TIP

Separate accounts or not, those small subscription fees we pay each month can begin to add up. Those video streaming services that are under twenty dollars, app subscriptions that may only be a few dollars, and other small expenses easily can go overlooked when bunched in with all your other transactions.

A good hack to avoid this is to have one separate account for those small expenses. We place our subscriptions on credit cards and review those statements every month to see if there's anything we need to cancel.

By doing this, it's easier to track everything. Otherwise, it could be several years down the road when you finally realize you are still paying for subscriptions you no longer use.

AUTOMATION

The process of separating your expenses into their own accounts is something that sounds great, right? Who doesn't like a little bit of organization in their life? But a common rebuttal we hear to this method is that the process of dividing up one's monthly income into these separate accounts can be time-consuming.

There's a trick, though. You can take out the mental part that comes with having to worry about budgeting. Freeing up mental space is why we're looking to automate our budget in the first place, isn't it? Think of a computer that runs slowly because it is trying to process so much information. That's your brain when you try to do all of this stuff manually.

Automating allows you to wipe that part clean. You can do a Control-Alt-Delete on your brain and close out all those programs running in the background, leaving all the room to focus on the programs you're actually using.

How do you do it? Use the tools you have at your disposal.

The beauty of paychecks today is that many companies offer direct deposit, which puts the money right into your bank account. But they also offer specific percentages of your direct deposit to be placed into separate accounts. This is your trick to automation.

Set up that direct deposit to break up your budgeted items for you. Does your budget include 5 percent of your income going to utility bills? Twenty percent going toward groceries and dining out? Create those separate bank accounts and then automate the rest by using direct deposit to put that certain percentage into each account.

Not only does this take out the labor of having to divide the money yourself, but it ensures your budget stays strictly intact. Run out of money in one of your accounts? Guess what? You'll have to wait until next month to visit that nice, new restaurant downtown, but your wallet will thank you for it.

Don't like that Plan? That's okay. You can choose to have all of your money direct deposited into a single account. That account can have rules in place that transfer amounts to subsequent accounts.

It's all in the planning. If you take some time at the beginning, you can use automation to open up more of your time to do the things you really want to.

YOUR AUTOMATED BUDGET

FLOWCHART

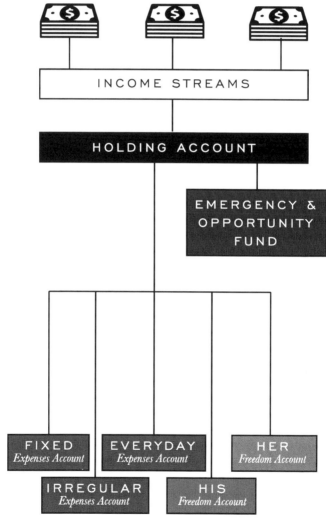

The ways in which budgeting can affect your financial life are so vast that an entire book could be written on the subject matter. And, in fact, many have. Probably dozens. Or hundreds. Who knows. But the idea behind all of these books is to make people realize just how important it is to budget.

Without a budget, you have no control over your finances. You become vulnerable to the little things that arise in your life and you make decisions based on what you have in your bank account at the moment rather than on what you need for the entire month. Essentially, you are giving up control of your money when you don't have a budget. You are instead handing over that control to the circumstances around you.

Think of a budget like a lock on the front door of your house. That lock gives you protection, and that's exactly what a budget does—it protects you from yourself. It protects you from the urges and impulse traps so many people fall into.

Not having a budget is like having a lock on your front door, but it's installed backwards. The lock is on the outside so anybody can come up, unlock it, and walk into your house. A backwards lock on your door serves no purpose.

Would you feel safe sleeping at night with a backwards lock on your front door? Would you feel protected? Of course you wouldn't. You would be up all night, tossing and turning and wondering if something bad was about to happen.

A budget protects you. It gives you control. It allows you to look into the future and see that everything will be fine and that you will have enough money to tap into those investments that will eventually set you free.

There's this stigma that surrounds budgeting where people relate the term to something constricting. They think of budgeting as some sort of restriction. They think, *That'll mean I have to reduce my lifestyle.*

When it comes to your money and the potential of living a financially free life, budgeting is the most critical starting point. It might not be the sexiest term or get the most attention among the investment community, but it's a necessary first step.

HOW QUICKLY DO YOU WANT TO GET THERE

The formula is **PI > ME**. You know this and you now have tactics to help move yourself toward Financial Freedom. But how quickly do you want to get there?

Nothing happens overnight. Financial freedom doesn't come with the flip of a switch. It's a process. And by keeping a budget and using budgeting hacks, you allow yourself to move closer to that freedom.

Without a budget, you are missing out on the cash-flowing opportunities that push your PI side higher. The time it will take to reach Financial Freedom becomes extended. Along the way, you may start to lose hope in the process.

On the other hand, having a budget and using strategic tactics puts a governor on your spending. It moves you closer toward independence in a reasonable amount of time.

FURTHER TACTICS

Budgeting is simply knowing your numbers. The Financial Scorecard that we created and that we share with our community members is an enhanced version of a budget—it has formulas already input to it and does the calculations for you—but your starting point can simply be writing down your income and expenses on a piece of paper.

From those numbers, allocate certain limits for each of your expenses and your hobbies. You will be amazed at how much clearer your financial situation becomes. Not only will this be the starting point to a new way of viewing your money, but it will allow you to know which investment paths are available to you. Those investment paths will be the doorway to a better future.

From there, mess around with the numbers a bit. See what feels right to you. See what potential opens up and then start to educate yourself on the available investment paths that will start generating passive income.

Want more budgeting tips? Check out our complete Automated Budget course.

www.wealthwithoutwallstreet.com/book

CHAPTER FIVE

BEING SMART WITH DEBT

"The wicked borrows but does not pay back, but the righteous is generous and gives."

—PSALM 37:21

There's a movie called *Cool Hand Luke* that was released in 1967. The overall plot of the story is that Luke, the main character, is sentenced to some time in prison but he doesn't always abide by all the rules while there. He's the rebel of the place, and in the process of becoming that rebel, the guards decide they're going to make his stay an unpleasant one.

The movie is not remembered for its plot or acting, but for a scene that, as we got older and, more importantly, deeper and deeper into educating ourselves on personal finance, became a great analogy for one thing:

Debt.

The scene in the movie starts off with Luke being called out by one of the prison guards after a long day of doing physical labor. Luke walks over to where he's summoned and the other prisoners nearby watch to see what's going on. Then the prison guard gives him a shovel, marks out a spot on the ground, and tells him to dig a hole.

In the scorching weather, he digs. He digs this hole in the ground and, as exhausted as he gets and as much as he wants to quit because he's so tired, he finishes. And then he climbs up and out of the hole thinking that he has won. The prison guard was trying to mentally break him by pushing him to a certain point and Luke wouldn't allow himself to be broken.

But then, as he's climbing out, another guard is standing there in the original one's place. This guard asks him, "Why are you digging a hole in my ground?" and makes him fill it back up. So he spends more time filling the hole, tired and struggling. And as he's almost done filling the hole, barely able to stand in the process, the original guard appears again.

"Why are you filling that hole? I told you to dig." And he tells Luke to dig the hole again.

You can imagine the frustration that character goes through, right? In the movie, he finally *does* hit his breaking point and he attacks one of the prison guards, which only results in his situation getting even worse.

Each of us reading that little piece can feel the character's frustration, yet few of us realize we are living out this exact scene over and over in our personal lives. It just comes in the form of debt instead of hard labor.

The first time you have to make a major purchase, you do so with debt. A car, a home, college education, or any other large expense is basically unobtainable unless you dig that hole and put yourself into debt. Then what do you do? What do basically *all* personal finance experts or gurus tell you to do? They tell you to pay off that debt, right? Pay it off as quickly as possible.

As you pay off that debt, you fill the hole. It takes a while and as you shovel in the dirt, scoop by scoop, you see progress along the way. When extra, unexpected money comes in, you throw it toward that debt because it's all you can think about—all you want to do is fill that hole and be done with it.

In time, you do. Congratulations! You can now drop the shovel and return back to your normal life.

But wait. Can you? Because, when you turn around and start walking away from that hole, other things start to appear. Life circumstances arise and there are other things that you suddenly need. Other things that came up while you were focusing solely on filling that hole.

Take your car, for example. Let's say you have a six-year loan and you do everything in your power to pay it off in four years—save a bit on interest, right? Sounds like a great idea, but as you focus solely on paying off that debt, other things accumulate. Maybe you desperately need some money to remodel your home. Or you get married during that time you're paying off your car and now your significant other needs a new one because theirs is putting around on its last leg.

In no time, you find yourself going back to that hole again, digging out the dirt. Once you dig it out, all you can think about is filling it back up again so you can have that fresh piece of land, like the hole was never there in the first place. But it never stays that way for long, does it? Because you will be running back to it. Digging.

Can you relate to this? Of course you can. We all can because we're pushed toward this idea of debt freedom. But debt freedom and Financial Freedom are not the same.

"Gurus" push debt freedom because it's emotional, which makes it an easy sell. They play into your emotions and sell you on their ideas, earning a profit in the process. You will never be able to pay off the cost of living. Should debt freedom really be the goal?

That's why our focus is on Financial Freedom. This not only forces you to consider monthly expenses and debt management, it also focuses on passive income production. Without passive income production, you will never be truly free. You will always need to work to pay off your bills.

DON'T USE THE SAME DIRT

You dig a hole, refill it, then run back to that same hole again when you need more money. Or worse, you start looking for other areas where you can dig a hole and before you know it, you're surrounded by holes and you don't have enough time or dirt to fill them all.

That's when you fall into a little thing called bankruptcy.

But think about this: what if you approached this whole idea of debt and consumption in a different way? What if you found your own little plot of land and instead of digging holes, you built mounds?

Interesting concept, right? Sure it is. Especially since it's different from the way the rest of the world thinks—the way we have been *trained* to think.

The key is not to continually use the same dirt to dig a hole and then refill it. To win in the game of finance, you need to start producing your own dirt. Find ways to invest in little areas around your plot of land that will produce mounds of soil. They might start small and you might need to continue going back to that same old hole for a little while, but in time, you will no longer need that initial place you have always had to run to. In time, as the needs for large purchases arise, you can begin to take from those growing piles.

You no longer need to be the indebted borrower of your loans. Instead, you are producing your own passive income that pays for the things you need. And do you want to know the best part? As you tap into those growing mounds of soil all around you, they will be replenished on their own using the same passive methods that allowed them to grow in the first place.

That's the beauty of cash flow.

INVESTING IN CASH FLOW VERSUS PAYING OFF DEBTS

Interest rates are a distraction. There, we said it.

How often do you find yourself looking at the interest rates you're paying on loans and judging the value of the loan based on that number? You're trying to figure out if you got the better end of the deal against the finance company but here's the secret: you never win. The lending company that loans you the money will always get the upper hand. They study the market and the economy and they know what they're doing.

They want you to feel as though you got a good deal with them, though. They want you to think you won so that you go back to them the next time you have to borrow.

That's where passively building your own mounds of dirt puts you in a great position. It gives you more freedom and then, you don't even need to focus on interest rates. Because you will have money consistently coming in that can cover the cost of *any* interest rate.

Look at Robert Kiyosaki, for example. If you're in the personal finance world, you have undoubtedly heard his name. If you haven't, his book *Rich Dad Poor Dad* is one of the most famous books in our field. It provides the most basic understanding of money and why finance isn't taught in schools.

Inside that book, though, Kiyosaki tells a story of buying his dream car, a 1989 Porsche. Now, for anyone focusing on their money and trying to attain wealth, buying a depreciating asset is a terrible idea. And cars are the most popular of all depreciating assets. They lose value as soon as you drive them off the lot and their value continually plummets from there. Compare that to an *appreciating* asset that puts money in your pocket and *increases* in value over time, and you can see why depreciating assets are bad.

But he bought his Porsche and it cost him nothing to do so. Want to know why? No, he didn't buy the car outright—he financed it. But he did so with passive cash flow that was coming into his pocket every month without him having to lift a finger to earn it. Instead of working enough hours each month to cover the car payment, he took some time to set up those passive income streams and then let them do the work for him.

As many people in the personal finance world say, *he put his money to work instead of working for his money.*

That's the key that so many people fail to realize: that you don't need to work for your money. It's why Wealth Without Wall Street was created—because most people are led to believe that the only way to accumulate wealth outside of your nine-to-five is to put your money into Wall Street. And that simply isn't true.

Take Russ's daughter, for example. When she was sixteen years old, she was getting her license and needed a car. With the $20,000 she had available in the whole life insurance policy that was set up for her (more on Infinite Banking in the next chapter), we set up an option where she could put her money to work in a short-term real estate rental. She put her money to work for her rather than working for her money. She was cash-flowing the $300 per month she needed for her car.

Her cousin, on the other hand, did what every other sixteen-year-old does when they want a car. She went out and got a job making $10 per hour. Let's do the math there, assuming the two would have the same car payment every month.

Russ's daughter: zero hours worked, $300 per month of passive income, car payment is paid.

Her cousin: Thirty hours worked per month, $0 of passive income, car payment is paid.

Now, we don't know about you, but we sort of like the idea of having our passive income paying our bills. Russ's daughter, compared to her cousin, had thirty extra hours available each month. She could do whatever she wanted with that time while her cousin was forced to work simply to pay for her car.

By creating your different avenues of passive income using the strategies we will explain in Step Three of this book, you too may find yourself one day behind the wheel of your dream car. But you need to step away from the idea of going back to that same hole you keep digging and refilling. Because if you get stuck in that cycle, it will be a difficult one to break.

GOOD DEBT VERSUS BAD DEBT

Now, we're going to do a little one eighty here and start talking about how debt can be used to your advantage. Because, yes, taking on debt can actually be a tool that helps you build your passive income streams.

We opened up the previous section with a bit of a head-scratcher: *interest rates are just a distraction.* And that's what they are here, too.

The world of personal finance teaches us to despise credit cards and other types of debt. Believe us, we couldn't agree more that borrowing money to buy consumer goods is a terrible idea. Like, maybe a big-screen TV while you're in college so you and your roommates can have a Super Bowl party.

Yes, there's a story behind that. Russ, in college, wanted to buy a big-screen TV for the party. But he had no credit so the store wouldn't sell him the $800 TV. His roommate, however, did have credit.

"If you buy this with your credit, I'll make all the payments." It sounds like a horrible decision but for two kids in college, it sounded wonderful. Russ certainly had his priorities in line.

His roommate agreed. The party took place. A three-hour football game played on the TV and then the party was over. But for many, many months after that party—about eighteen, in fact—Russ made monthly payments on that television.

Eighteen months had passed and Russ had moved out of the house. He still made the payments, though, and he called up his former roommate to ask how much he still owed on the bill. *It has to be close to the $800 by now*, he thought.

"I called. They said there's still a balance of $762."

A year and a half of payments and only $38 had been removed from the principal balance. That was Russ's first lesson on consumer debt—*bad debt*.

Think about all the money Russ paid in interest payments over that eighteen-month period.

$$\$50 \text{ per month} \times 18 \text{ months of payments}$$
$$= \$900 \text{ paid to the store for that TV}$$

Think about some of your own bad decisions with consumer debt. How much extra money have you paid toward something that has brought you no monetary gain in return?

Good debt, on the other hand, can be acquired in the same manner. Personal loans and credit cards get some bad hype in the personal finance world, but they can be used for good. Mainly, if they are used to purchase an appreciating asset.

Here's an example. Here at Wealth Without Wall Street, we're all about real estate rentals. Short-term or long-term, we don't really care. They're both great ways to start making passive income while increasing your net worth at the same time. Many people find it difficult to break into real estate, though, because they don't have that up-front capital needed for the initial down payment. When it comes to investment properties, you need that 20 percent down to get inside the house.

What if you don't have it? Is borrowing a bad idea?

Maybe, maybe not. Let's look at an example of how borrowing could open up the potential for monthly cash flow while also gaining equity in the house every month. Granted, you will need a tenant in place to get either of those things, but if you can have a tenant lined up, that's a positive indication.

The tool you need to open up the chance of landing that cash flow opportunity is cash. If it has to be borrowed with interest, is that bad? Well, let's see.

Say the house you want to purchase is for sale for $75,000. You need a $15,000 down payment and you only have $5,000 available. You would need to borrow the additional $10,000 on a personal loan that would cost you roughly $161 per month for the next ten years at 15 percent.

On the surface, taking on a loan that costs $161 per month seems like additional debt, right? But hold on a minute, because by taking on this debt, you have now enabled yourself to purchase the rental home. And you can charge $900 per month for rent on this home.

Now, is it worth it? Let's see:

Rental Income	$900
Mortgage Payment on the Remaining $60,000 Balance	– $322
Personal Loan Payment on the $10,000	– $161
Property Taxes and Insurance	– $150
Gross Profit before Management Fee and Reserves	= $267

But that's only the gross profit. Now we need to calculate some of the other management fees.

Gross Profit	$267
Monthly Property Management Fee	– $90
Monthly Maintenance Reserve	– $90
Monthly Vacancy Reserve	– $75
Net Profit	= $12

By taking on that $10,000 loan for the down payment, you have enabled yourself to create $12 per month of passive cash flow. But don't forget about one other component of this deal: you are gaining equity in that home free of charge—nothing comes out of your pocket. The rent payments are being allocated toward those mortgage payments and you, as the home's owner, are gaining equity.

That's good debt. It's debt that can actually *make* you money. Or at the very least, increase your net worth.

Want to see good debt on steroids? Chapter Six on the Infinite Banking Concept should get you excited.

KEEP EMOTION OUT OF YOUR DECISIONS

We're all emotional beings. God didn't put us on this green earth to be boring, robotic, unemotional creatures, now did he? That's what makes us so special.

However, this emotion that we carry with us can cause us to make irrational decisions. This is especially true when it comes to our money. If you have an emotional connection to your debt, the chances of you making an ill-informed decision become much greater.

Paying off your debts as quickly as possible is one of the first places people turn when it comes to emotional decision-making. They think that by getting their debts paid off faster, they will be closer to being financially free.

But there's a lot more to it. As our *Cool Hand Luke* analogy will tell you, filling that hole faster won't prevent you from having to dig it up again. In fact, it usually just means you will be redigging that hole again sooner than you would have if you had just taken your time and begun building dirt mounds around you.

Think about all of life's scenarios that pop up. Holidays, school events for your kids, unexpected doctor's visits or illnesses—the list goes on. These are things that simultaneously pull dirt from your hole as you continue digging. Not to mention, the second you stop to take a break, dirt is being thrown in in the form of these normal life events.

Feeling overwhelmed? You're not alone. Emotion makes us all think about our debt and want to try as hard as we can to get rid of it. Debt all seems bad. But it isn't going anywhere. It costs money to live. You either end up working your entire life, chasing after the money to pay those bills, or you begin creating passive income.

Here's a story you might relate to. One of our coaches

worked with a client recently who was unsure how to allocate his money. He knew he wanted to get rid of his debt so he worked hard to do so. Ever hear of people making additional payments toward the principal of their mortgage? Well this guy was paying *triple his monthly mortgage payment* in an attempt to get rid of his debt faster. Triple!

Our coach worked with him and told him that yes, he might be free of that debt in ten or fifteen years. But what happens next? What happens when the mortgage is paid off? Is life free then? Can he quit his job and stop paying bills?

Of course not. Although the house is paid off, he still needs to pay property tax. He needs to pay for his electricity, water, and internet. He will still need to work to pay for these things if he continues aggressively paying off his mortgage.

The coach he worked with introduced him to the idea of using that extra monthly cash to invest in passive income streams. In ten or fifteen years, he actually could be financially free, with enough cash coming in to pay all of his bills, not just his mortgage.

This was a shock to him. It was the opposite of what he had always thought was the right move—paying off debt as quickly as possible.

If you're a person who is emotional with their money, this chapter has probably driven you crazy thus far. We have discussed ways debt can be used to increase your passive income but if you like things simplified and you just want a clear head, free from debt, what we've discussed probably isn't for you.

Yet, when has thinking emotionally ever done us any good? Mixing emotions with money is bad. When it comes to spending, investing, borrowing, or any other measure of our money, practical thinking is what's important. It's the *practical* decisions that will get you to where you want to go, not the *emotional* ones.

Emotions create limitations whereas practical thinking can create abundance. Remember that the next time you hear someone say the word *debt*. Don't allow it to be a word that limits you. Don't run away and hide from it.

WHICH WAY IS THE DECISION MOVING YOU?

Are you moving closer to Financial Freedom or farther away? This is the most important thing to realize as you move forward and make your decisions.

Look, keeping emotions out of decision-making is tough. We completely understand. We've been there. Heck, Russ made payments on a TV for *years* just so he could have a Super Bowl party. If that's not an emotional act, then what is?

This is why we use a framework. We know emotions take over easily and often. So we created a Priority Payoff Guide for our community and our clients. It has helped us to think practically about our decisions and we have seen it help others have a clear vision on their journey to Financial Freedom.

Practical thinking will get you to where you need to be. Whether it's paying off bad debts, using money on hand to create new debts, or any other form of investing that pushes you closer to that overall end result, you should always be thinking about the future.

If you need some guidance in doing so, we have put together a Priority Payoff Guide that helps you determine which of your debts you should be paying off first. Visit the link below to access the free guide.

www.wealthwithoutwallstreet.com/book

CHAPTER SIX

INFINITE BANKING CONCEPT (IBC)

"For where your treasure is, there your heart will be also."

—MATTHEW 6:21

Our bread and butter. Our heart and soul. This is where our worlds collided. It's where the two of us slowly moved our friendship into a business partnership, because we both found so much value in this idea of the Infinite Banking Concept, or IBC.

So what is it? And where did the idea for the concept come to us?

It was in January of 2009 when the book *Becoming Your Own Banker* by R. Nelson Nash was introduced to Russ at a conference for CPAs and Financial Professionals. The financial crisis was in full bloom and the author was telling a room full of financial professionals how they could allow their clients to control the banking function in their life.

On a short flight home to Birmingham from Orlando, Russ

read the entire book. He couldn't put it down. The book walked him through the unknown benefits of dividend-paying whole life insurance. It was an introduction to a financial instrument that Russ hadn't been aware of—because it didn't fit into the model financial advisors were taught to follow.

To that point, Russ had been led to believe 401(k) plans and Individual Retirement Accounts (IRAs) were the only methods for retirement. He, like everyone else, was led into the arms of Wall Street. And then *Becoming Your Own Banker* came along and ripped the rug out from beneath him. It was inspiring. Enlightening. And it changed Russ's stance on financial freedom forever.

One section in particular caught his eye: the detailed explanation of how banks make money by using their depositors' money. Everyone knows how this works, but to Russ, the ways around keeping your money in the bank were eye-opening.

Right around this time, in February of 2009, his wife, Megan, was opening a dental practice. As a licensed dentist, she was excited about the idea. But she needed money. So she went to the number one dental practice lender in the country: Bank of America.

There were a lot of negatives in the stock market during this time. We, like most others, thought banks were financially stable institutions before those events. And when it came to stock market investments—well before Wealth Without Wall Street, mind you—there were few better guarantees than banks and their stock prices.

It was for this reason that Megan's father went to Russ, his son-in-law and financial advisor, and entrusted him to invest his retirement savings. The task was completed, without question, and the one safe bet where all the retirement money was invested was to one bank: Bank of America.

The crash caused Bank of America's stock to fall. It hurt Russ's father-in-law's retirement savings, but not to an extent it could have. When the orders were initially placed, Russ initiated what's called a *stop-loss order*, effectively ensuring that the losses wouldn't go any lower than 15 percent.

When the crash took place, the stop-loss order kicked in, automatically selling his father-in-law's shares. In the end, the total amount her father-in-law had gotten back was around $950,000. And, ironically, he placed it into an account with the same bank whose stocks he had just sold: Bank of America.

You see where this is going?

After reading *Becoming Your Own Banker*, seeing $950,000 go into a Bank of America and a loan come out of that same bank for $700,000, something clicked. Now, neither of us will claim to be the smartest person in the room, in *any* room we're in, but this just seemed pretty simple.

The loan for the dental practice came with an interest rate of 7.95 percent. That interest rate had to be paid and it was the bank's way of profiting. At the same time, his father-in-law's money was going to be used to fund loans for the bank.

In our situation, both Megan *and* her father were allowing the bank to make a profit. Again, no claim to be a genius here, but the writing on the wall was pretty clear. What if we used the $950,000 to fund the $700,000 loan? The loan gets approved and interest can be made without the bank getting involved. A win–win for both sides.

This is where Infinite Banking comes into play. It can be a life-altering concept if used properly. It's one that we help nearly all of our clients with and one that we have used to create wealth for ourselves and our families. And with the information that's in the pages to come, you will soon be able to do the same.

But first, more about those money-hungry banks.

A BANK'S ASSET SHEET

Want to hear some numbers that could make you sick? Bank of America, one of the largest banks in the nation, took in $860 billion worth of deposits in 2017. Off of that, they earned 5.2 percent in interest payments. Do the math there and it will tell you that in a single year, Bank of America earned an income of just under $45 billion. And that's just in interest payments.

Think about that. Using *your* money—your bank deposits—to lend to others, they created $45 billion in income *in a single year*.

Here's some questions for you: When you drive through any major city and you look up at those tall buildings, what do you see? What are the names that line the tops of those tall, expensive buildings?

Banks, right? Think about that. Think of all the cities across America. We're talking major cities, minor cities, and mini little high-rises in tiny suburban towns. All over the nation, without fail, these banks find ways to get their name in front of you. Not to mention, they have branches and ATMs located on every corner.

Why is that? Well, it's simple: they want you to be consistently reminded that they're there. That they are available. Not only that, but they want you to see just how big and important they are. Because if you, the potential bank client, see a bank name everywhere you go, you're going to assume they're doing something right—that they're good at handling money. And if they're good at handling money, they will be good at handling *your* money.

So they try to swallow up all this real estate in hopes that the constant reappearance of their name encourages you to pull into the parking lot and to bank with them.

It's not a bad Plan. Robert Kiyosaki talks about this in *Rich*

Dad Poor Dad. He talks about the owner of McDonald's, Ray Kroc, and how he would always tell people that McDonald's is in the real estate business, not in the restaurant business. If you think about it, he's right. Every McDonald's you see is in a prime location.

Banks have the same model, only they pay a lot more money to get their names onto those high-rises across the country. So between all the bank branches they have and all of those skyline buildings displaying their name, you would think that the number one asset class they have is real estate. There's no way that they could put more money into anything else, could they?

Well, let's see.

Take a look at the following image.

WELLS FARGO BANK NATIONAL ASSOCIATION

101 N. Phillips Avenue, Sioux Falls, SD 57104 | FDIC Certificate #: 3511 | Bank Charter Class: N

Definition	Wells Fargo Bank, National Association Sioux Falls, SD December 31, 2020	Wells Fargo Bank, National Association Sioux Falls, SD December 31, 2019
Assets and Liabilities		
1. Total employees (full-time equivalent)	233,403	232,982
2. **Total Assets**	**1,767,808,000**	**1,712,919,000**
3. Cash and due from depository institutions	246,223,000	140,263,000
4. Interest-bearing balances	218,658,000	119,085,000
5. Securities	417,233,000	405,807,000
6. Federal funds sold and reverse repurchase agreements	58,404,000	60,412,000
7. Net loans and leases	872,025,000	934,435,000
8. Bank premises and fixed assets	**11,262,000**	**11,822,000**
9. Goodwill and other intangibles	30,307,000	36,032,000
10. All other assets	62,522,000	62,670,000
11. Total liabilities and capital	1,767,808,000	1,712,919,000
12. Total liabilities	1,596,880,000	1,545,526,000
13. Total deposits	1,479,499,000	1,382,138,000
14. Interest-bearing deposits	935,175,000	982,307,000
15. Deposits held in domestic offices	1,443,370,000	1,326,735,000
16. % insured	50.66%	49.05%
17. Federal funds purchased & repurchase agreements	8,224,000	9,876,000
18. Trading liabilities	15,639,000	9,458,000
19. Other borrowed funds	48,157,000	100,635,000
20. Subordinated debt	12,350,000	11,937,000
21. All other liabilities	33,011,000	31,482,000
22. Total equity capital	170,928,000	167,393,000
23. Total bank equity capital	170,894,000	167,346,000
24. Perpetual preferred stock	0	0
25. Common stock	519,000	519,000
26. Surplus	114,820,000	114,728,000
27. Undivided profits	55,555,000	52,099,000
28. Noncontrolling interests in consolidated subsidiaries	34,000	47,000
Memoranda:		
29. Noncurrent loans and leases	17,224,000	13,415,000
30. Noncurrent loans that are wholly or partially guaranteed by the U.S. government	8,119,000	7,260,000
31. Income earned, not collected on loans	4,278,000	5,091,000
32. Earning assets	1,611,594,000	1,567,340,000
33. Long-term assets (5+ years)	609,133,000	605,270,000
34. Average Assets, year-to-date	1,758,911,800	1,695,685,800
35. Average Assets, quarterly	1,759,002,000	1,710,733,500
36. Life insurance assets	**19,298,000**	*18,999,000*
37. Separate account life insurance assets	13,013,000	12,998,000
38. Hybrid life insurance assets	632,000	619,000
39. Volatile liabilities	79,092,000	138,820,000
40. Insider Loans	9,000	110,000
41. FHLB advances	32,000	25,491,000
42. Loans and leases held for sale	34,944,000	16,488,000
43. Unused loan commitments	599,349,000	584,148,000
44. Tier 1 (core) risk-based capital	150,168,000	145,149,000
45. Tier 2 risk-based capital	23,551,000	20,907,000
46. Total unused commitments	599,349,000	584,148,000
47. Derivatives	8,862,751,000	12,057,979,000
Total assets and liabilities in foreign offices		
Restructured loans and leases		
Past due and nonaccrual assets		
Fiduciary and related services		*All numbers are in thousands.*

This is Wells Fargo Bank's balance sheet from 2019. Since they are a publicly traded company, this information is available to anybody who wants it. It's a financial document that the executives at Wells Fargo release for everyone to see.

Find the row labeled *bank premises and fixed assets* and then slide your finger across the page and take a look at those numbers. Big numbers, right? They are. But we know why their real estate holdings are so large—it's for the reasons we have been discussing so far.

Now look farther down the page. Find the row labeled *cash value life insurance* and look at the number associated with *that* asset class. Wow, look at that—they have more money put into their life insurance assets than they do in real estate. Everything we've been discussing about the importance of real estate to banks, yet they put more money into life insurance policies than they do into all of that property.

Here's another number for you: two-thirds of banks in the US own BOLI, or bank-owned life insurance. As of 2021, this totaled roughly $183 billion.

So what does this all mean? Why are we talking about prime real estate and asset classes for banks?

Think about the transfer of money between us and the banks where we deposit. We get our paycheck, we instantly hand it over to the bank, and then the bank puts the money either right into real estate—no surprise there—or into life insurance policies.

The solution is simple: cut out the middleman.

AN INTRODUCTION TO IBC

The idea surrounding IBC is that there has to be a way that we, the individual, can regain control. For so long, we have been led to believe that we need to be separated from our money. When our paychecks come in, we're encouraged to accelerate the pay-down of our mortgages and auto loans, max out our retirement accounts...basically, anywhere that we don't have complete control.

Then what happens? We have all these things in life that we need—heck, even things that we *want*—and we don't have the money to buy them. Our money is now divided up into so many different areas and some of those areas don't allow us to pull out that cash right away when we need it.

So what do we do? When situations arise where we need to make a large purchase, we go right to the banks that convinced us it was a good idea to give them our money. Then we apply for a loan and the determining factor as to whether or not they will loan us the money is up to them. Loan terms, financing, and approvals are all in their control.

With IBC, *you* have the ability to take back that control. You no longer need to run to the banks to ask for some of your money back. You create your own loans because you have your own cash value, just like the banks do.

When an investment opportunity comes along, you have the ability to take advantage of it. Having access to cash forces you to become a better investor, while giving up access to all your money makes you dependent on others.

Infinite Banking, in short, is the idea of becoming your own banker by utilizing the cash accumulation within specifically designed whole life insurance policies. When most people hear *life insurance*, they think of *term* life insurance. They think of that small monthly payment that protects them in the event they should pass away within the allotted time frame—the *term* of the policy.

Term life insurance policies are meant to be safety nets.

They can protect your loved ones in the event that you die and your income completely cuts off. Term Insurance policies provide a Death Benefit so they are good for protection, but many people scoff at the idea as a scam because you could pay into the policy for twenty, thirty, or even forty years and get nothing in return.

Whole life insurance policies operate much differently. Unlike term policies that provide protection only for a specified time (ten, twenty years, etc.), whole life policies are designed to offer you protection throughout your lifetime. These policies can pay out dividends, which increase cash value and create income, but they also provide that desired death benefit. The best part about these policies, though, is they can borrow against the cash value of the policy, not the value of the policy, without having to go through the credit check process, fill out loan paperwork, or any of the other headaches involved with traditional loans.

How is this possible? Simple. It's because the money in the policy is yours. You've paid into it, similar to creating equity in your house through principal payments on your mortgage. Instead of splitting up your paycheck into checking, savings, and retirement accounts, you have put it into a whole life insurance policy that holds a cash value.

Think about the circumstances in your life when emergencies arise and you could really use a loan. Yet when those circumstances come up, you're typically in a tight spot financially, which means traditional lenders won't give you the time of day and the money in your retirement accounts aren't accessible. If you have a whole life insurance policy, all you have to do is pick up the phone and ask to tap into a certain amount of your policy's cash value.

HOW WHOLE LIFE INSURANCE POLICIES WORK

There are studies that show that only about 2 percent of term life insurance policies ever actually pay out, which means that 98 percent of people who pay into term policies never see a penny out of it. So why do we do it? It's that bargain shopper in us that wants to pay the least amount possible for the greatest possible result. And with term life policies costing only twenty or thirty bucks a month and paying out over $100,000 or more, that's a pretty good gamble.

But insurance companies know what they're doing. They have hundreds of years of data to calculate the actual costs and expected death rate. They have created an entire business around it. These companies calculate what it would cost to pay for the 2 percent of death claims as well as paying their business expenses and taking a profit off of that. They take no risk. Everything is calculated.

When it comes to the death benefit, whole life insurance policies have a similar structure. It's the added value that makes these policies so great, though. Because they are more than just security blankets protecting your family in the event something should happen to you—they are also warehouses for available cash.

The way we structure policies for ourselves and for our clients is that we only buy policies that are dividend-paying contracts with mutual life insurance companies.

Okay, so what do each of these terms mean? The first—dividend-paying—means that dividends are paid to each policyholder based on the success of the insurance company. It works the same as dividend-paying stocks or private businesses, where a successful fiscal quarter is met with payments to shareholders. Only in this case, the dividend payments go to the policyholder: you.

The second term—contract—is a guarantee or agreement that is legally binding. When these whole life insurance companies guarantee a specific return in their contract, they are legally bound to provide it. What contract does your 401(k) provider have with you in regard to the returns in your mutual funds?

The third term—the mutual insurance company—means that the company is owned by the policyholders, not by private shareholders or investors. So as someone who purchases a Plan with a mutual insurance company, you are also buying ownership in the company.

If you have any familiarity with banks versus credit unions, the differentiation is the same—credit unions are owned by the account holders while banks are owned by private investors or those who buy shares on the stock market. So if you ever hear, "Oh, that insurance company is ripping you off," that can't necessarily be true if it's owned by its policyholders.

With these policies, the death benefit many of us seek in a life insurance policy begins from day one. You can sleep soundly knowing your family is safe in the event something happens to you. You can also be satisfied in knowing that as long as your premium payments are made on time, your cash value will continue to grow alongside those premiums.

Then there's the paid-up additions, which can open up all sorts of possibilities. With the paid-up additions rider, you can pump more cash into the policy in order to set yourself up for greater dividend payments and a greater cash value.

And it's this cash value that makes Infinite Banking such a great financial framework. Think of it as buying a home and building equity in that home over time. *That's* Infinite Banking.

A lot has been covered in this section, we know. There's more to come, too. It's a complicated subject matter but one that can change the outcome of your future if used correctly. So we're offering our IBC 101 Course for free since you purchased this book. Grab the link to the course from our Resources List at www.wealthwithoutwallstreet. com/book. See that? You're making smarter financial moves already.

If you follow along easier with video and audio, this might help. But we still encourage you to read through this chapter to get the basic understanding.

GETTING STARTED WITH IBC

Okay, so you can earn dividends and can put your money into an insurance company owned by its policyholders. But who cares? What's the big deal about these policies and what do they have to do with Infinite Banking?

We want to invest. We want to invest in ourselves, and in passive income streams. We want to utilize the cash that we put into these policies so that we can create cash flow in other areas. Infinite Banking provides that opportunity and does so with you in the driver's seat.

To be in the proverbial driver's seat, you need to have a proverbial car—the whole life policy. This means you need to open that account. You need to find that mutual life insurance company and research what they have to offer and how their policies work. At Wealth Without Wall Street, this is one of the major time-saving services we provide because we have been partnering with several companies since 2009 and we know their contracts inside and out.

However, as long as you find a licensed IBC practitioner, you should be in good hands. And that doesn't mean simply setting up a basic account. There are structures that need to be put in place in order to maximize the value of your contract. You won't find this policy design at your local insurance agency. You need specific, trained professionals to help you—those who practice this very process on a regular basis. If not, you could end up having a bad experience and could put yourself years behind in the process.

That's not said to scare you. It's said to emphasize the importance.

INVESTING WITH IBC

With the policy started and an initial deposit secured, you now have a death benefit in place. Congratulations! You have what most people who purchase life insurance policies strive for.

Now comes the fun part: the investment portion of the Plan.

A good way to think about your whole life policy and its investments is to think about the fuel usage of an airplane. If you're unfamiliar, planes use a lot more fuel at the beginning of their trip than at the end. Taking off burns a ton of fuel but so too does the first leg of the flight. Why? Because that full tank of fuel is weighing down the plane. As the engines burn the fuel, the tank empties, the plane becomes lighter, and the fuel efficiency continues to improve throughout the flight.

R. Nelson Nash uses a similar analogy in *Becoming Your Own Banker*. He tells his readers to picture cutting open a tree and seeing the rings inside that represent years of the tree's growth. The smallest rings—those in the middle—represent the tree in its earliest days. And as more and more rings of the tree are added, the tree grows wider. Essentially, the older the tree, the fatter the trunk, and the more rings inside when you cut it open. That is something that can only happen with time.

The same applies to whole life policies and the cash value that grows within them. When your policy first begins, you *do* have that death benefit, but you won't have that full cash value to borrow against. That portion takes a little while to build up.

However, with a *paid-up additions* rider added to your policy, you can grow the trunk of your tree a whole lot faster than you would if you simply let it grow on its own. By contributing paid-up additions each year, you are accelerating the cash value of the Plan.

In a typical scenario, when someone buys a whole life policy from a life insurance agent it might look something like this:

They purchase a large death benefit for their $1,000 per month insurance premium. After three to four years, the $1,000 per month premium starts to create a cash value. At that rate, it might take a few decades, but they will eventually get to the point where their cash value equals their contributions and could be a good source of cash reserves.

However, with a paid-up additions rider, you can add additional money to the contract that purchases very small amounts of death benefit and, hence, can add immediate cash value to be accessed.

To demonstrate the example, take the same policy with the $1,000 per month premium. That policy could allow for an additional $2,000 to $3000 per month paid-up additions rider to be added. This would allow for a large percentage of the monthly premium to not only be available to be accessed, but also would allow the premiums to equal the cash value at a much faster pace. This gives you access to borrow against that money sooner, opening up the potential to borrow from yourself and to invest in the process.

And the paid-up additions rider is only *one* of the many financial benefits.

THE MONEY ON TOP OF THE MONEY

As one of our trusted Wealth Without Wall Street coaches says, "Infinite Banking allows you to have one dollar doing three jobs at once."

Imagine the two of us approached you on the street one day and handed you a one dollar bill. First, you'd probably roll your eyes at us for only handing over a single dollar bill to you. But then you would think to yourself, *What am I going to do with this?*

It's a single dollar. You can't split it up. So you carry on with your day, and as you do, you continue to walk around. You look into the windows of small shops, you pass by a few department stores, and you can't figure out what you'll spend this dollar on.

Then it hits you: *I shouldn't spend this money. I should put it away somewhere. Invest it. Allow this dollar bill to go to work for me and make me money.* But where? You only have a single dollar bill. It can only be in one place at one time.

Do you invest it where it earns a fraction of a percent in interest or somewhere that allows it to earn 5 or 6 percent in interest? Do you want it to be taxed when you take it out or do you want it tax-free? And do you want it to be locked away, untouchable until retirement, or do you want it to be *liquid*, meaning it is easily accessible?

Why not all three? Remember, *Infinite Banking allows you to have one dollar doing three jobs at once.* If you take that dollar and place it into a whole life policy, you have immediate life insurance, immediate cash value that you can use to put into investment paths like real estate or business ventures, and you can also watch as the money grows consistently through dividends and compounding.

Investing the money in passive income streams also allows you to collect earnings through those investments. What can you do with those earnings? You can spend them, sure, but why not reinvest them into a new IBC policy so *that* money can start doing three jobs at once, also?

Where else do you get this kind of versatility in a savings Plan? We'll tell you where: nowhere. That's why this has been the framework around Wealth Without Wall Street and has given us, our team members, and our clients the ability to create passive income streams that will continue to grow for a long time.

If you're looking for a downfall here, there's only one thing that could possibly be noted as a con, and that's the time it takes to build your cash value to the place you want it to be. There are other, quicker ways to get cash for investments and significant purchases, but they don't come with any of the benefits IBC brings.

There's no getting around the fact that it takes some time to build these policies to where they become consistent sources of cash. But if you have the patience and utilize paid-up additions, you will find yourself in a much better financial situation in just a few years' time.

Again, IBC is a process. And processes take time to perfect. Small adjustments need to be made here and there to make sure everything is being utilized to maximum efficiency.

Here's the challenge, though. You have to think about this differently than you've ever thought about a financial process or product before. As our mentor Nelson Nash said, "If you knew at passive income time (his word for "retirement"—*ha!*) that you would be getting back everything you paid into a system, tax-free, would you object to putting more money in?"

What other process do you know that will do this? On top of that, what other process will do this while also outliving you for generations to come?

PRODUCT VERSUS PROCESS

We're intertwining the terms Infinite Banking and whole life policy here because they go hand in hand, but they *are* different from one another. The key differentiator is that one is a product while the other is a process.

Whole life is a product—a financial *product*. It is a life insurance policy and a tool that can be used to provide a permanent death benefit to your family and a cash value to be used as a cash reserve.

The concept of Infinite Baking is a *process*. It is the process of controlling the flow of your money. It's a personal cash flow system. Now, this process can actually be performed without a whole life policy. But when you think about the fact that you need access to money to finance the purchases in life, then the money has to be liquid. So when comparing this process to something more common, it has to be relatable to a checking account, savings account, or some other form of liquid, available cash.

IBC cannot be compared to other investment strategies like stocks, bonds, or retirement accounts because these limit access to your money—they're *illiquid*. That money is tied up in whichever avenue you put it in until the people managing your money say, "Okay, you can have it back now."

Again, IBC is a process. And processes take time to perfect. They need small adjustments made here and there to make sure everything is being utilized to maximum efficiency.

We've done this. Between the dozens of policies we have

set up for ourselves, our family, and our employees, and the thousands more we have helped clients to initiate, we know the process inside and out. This process has allowed us to create over $65,000 per month in passive income, create numerous businesses, and more importantly, provide a pool of cash where our children and our children's children will never have to use a bank in their lives.

In the real-life example of Megan and her dental practice, the loan her father took out against his own whole life policy allowed his cash to grow guaranteed, let him earn the interest that the bank would have otherwise made from the loan, as well as build an asset that Megan would ultimately inherit at his passing.

IBC doesn't only have to be about compounding your money through dividends or tapping into the cash value to invest in an amazing asset like real estate. It can be used to help family members. Help friends. Give some new business you like the startup money they need to get off the ground.

With IBC, *you* are in control, not the bank. That's a tough idea for many to believe but once you see the potential for opportunities for your cash flow to increase every month by becoming your own banker, the world will open up for you. Now all you have to do is concentrate on ways to keep Uncle Sam's hands out of your pockets.

CHAPTER SEVEN

TAXES

"Then he said to them, 'Therefore render to Caesar the things that are Caesar's, and to God the things that are God's.'"

—MATTHEW 22:21

What's your single largest expense? The one that takes the most out of your pocket every month without providing some sort of financial return. Is it your mortgage? Rent? Your car payment?

These are the top three answers we receive when we ask the question. Yet while these are all some of the top contributors to our personal expense column, none of these options is the true answer.

The answer is taxes.

Robert Kiyosaki summed it up perfectly when he said, "It's not about how much money you *make*, it's about how much money you *keep*." This is why tax strategists have jobs—to save money for people who would otherwise turn it over to the government.

Let's come up with yet another scenario, shall we? We know this book is loaded with them but they help paint the picture. So let's throw ourselves into another one.

Imagine yourself as a ten-year-old wanting to start a paper

route. It's a dated reference, we get it, but let's stick with it. As a ten-year-old, you want to start a paper route so you go to your grandma and ask to borrow one hundred dollars from her. She gives it to you, of course, because it's Grandma and she thinks it's adorable that you're trying to start your own little business.

In one year's time, you surprise Grandma. You let her know that your company grew by 20 percent that year and that your expectations are to grow another 20 percent the following year.

And again, you surprise her. Year over year, this little business of yours takes off and you grow the business by 20 percent every year. In one hundred years, you have handed down your business to your children and your grandchildren, and the business is booming now. That initial one hundred dollar investment, growing at 20 percent year over year for one hundred years, is now worth $8,281,797,452. One heck of a growth trajectory.

But we can't forget Uncle Sam's cut of the deal. To make things simple, let's say we're put into a 30 percent tax bracket over this hundred-year span. How much of that $8,281,797,452 do you think would be left over during that one-hundred-year run if taxed annually at 30 percent?

Did you guess $49 million? Yes, you read that right—*million*. The total profit dropped from nearly 8.3 *billion* to only 49 *million* when the 30 percent tax bracket was brought into the equation.

So wait a minute. Does that mean the entire difference went to the government? Did the government actually profit $8.2 billion over the course of your one hundred years in business?

Not quite. In fact, they only made $21 million in total over that time period.

Okay. There are a lot of numbers being thrown at you here and we know that a lot of them aren't making sense. How does 30 percent in taxes make $8.2 billion just up and disappear? And how does the government only end up with $21 million after all that? What happened to all those billions of dollars? Where did they go?

Confusing stuff, we know. However, there's a really simple explanation for this. It's called the Laffer Curve.

THE LAFFER CURVE

The largest eroder of money in this country is taxes. It *eliminates* money.

You saw how compounding worked in the paper route scenario. Compounding, which is like continuously stacking poker chips year over year and watching the mound grow taller and wider, turned a single hundred dollar bill into $8.3 billion. This is proof that, if uninterrupted, money can accumulate significantly. It's when we tax it that the issues arise.

When we talk about taxes, they are the biggest expense in one's life, but they are also the heaviest weight holding us back from creating the wealth we desire. What we need to do to remove this limitation is to legally look for ways to *not* pay taxes.

Notice, we said *legally*. We want to avoid taxes, not evade them. The difference between the two is about a twenty-five-year prison sentence.

Okay, now we're about to get into some tax talk here that might strike some people as political jargon. Your stance on taxes and who should pay what might seem like it's coming into question, but it isn't. Your political affiliations and beliefs on who should pay what aren't what we're about to discuss. What we're discussing is the real, tangible change that occurs when taxes are adjusted.

There is always talk of increasing taxes on the rich and using that money to benefit those who are in need. The Robin Hood effect. In some circles, this is deemed to be the proper thing for governments to do—equal the playing field, if you will. However, let's take a look at the numbers when we consider taxing the rich.

Take the $21 million carried over from the prior example. That's what the government would have made at the tax rate of 30 percent. If that tax rate is increased to 40 percent, what do you think happens to the total amount of money the government would make over that one-hundred-year span? It would go up, right? I mean, it only makes sense—higher tax rate leads to more money.

Not quite. When the math is done, the total tax collected over that century now falls from $21 million to $5.5 million.

What? How did that happen? How is that even possible?

This is what the Laffer Curve explains.

THE LAFFER CURVE

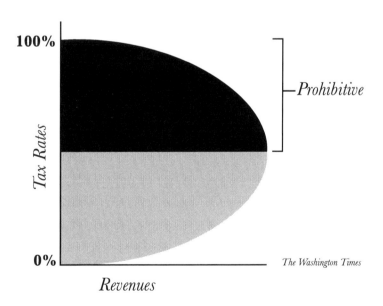

The Laffer Curve was designed by Art Laffer, a member of the Reagan administration and former economics professor at the University of Chicago. He designed this in 1940 as a way of putting a visualization to the tax process. What this curve shows is that there is a perfect tax rate that allows governments to collect the most tax revenue without going too high or too low.

TAXES AND (YOUR) BUSINESS

We'd like to take a moment right here to point out that neither of us is a tax attorney, nor are we certified or professional accountants. Our area of expertise is cash flow and while we've been researching our area of expertise, we have come across some sensible ways to increase cash flow by way of tax strategies.

Most of these methods are commonly used by the most successful people in the United States. However, they are fairly uncommon to the rest of us. But it doesn't have to be this way. We all have access to the use of the same tax code, helping you save on your tax bill each year.

BE A BUSINESS

The Laffer Curve has a lot to do with tax revenue based on the government's role in setting rates, but it doesn't tell the story of the individual's tax implications—*your* tax burden. This can only be dictated by the decisions you make throughout the year and how you allocate your money.

One of the simplest things you can do is to set yourself up as a legal business structure rather than collecting your income as an individual. The government gives tax breaks to businesses and corporations.

If businesses had higher tax rates and were discouraged

from creating new jobs, the tax revenue for the government would shrink. So our government incentivizes business owners and investors who create more wealth by creating more jobs and more opportunity for people to earn a paycheck.

It is for this reason that you should consider setting yourself up as a business. If you're an employee of an organization, this might not be an option for you. But if you're doing work on your own as a contractor or freelancer, this is something that could save you money down the line. Not only is your tax bill lower, but the business structure you choose could allow you to move money around in methods favorable to your taxes.

Take an LLC, for example—a limited liability corporation. It is a simple organization that many businesses choose to create. The main, non-tax-related reason is that an LLC can protect you in the event of a lawsuit. If you were to be sued for any reason for work done under your own name, you could lose everything—everything that has your name on it. That could be your house, your car, and even your business. But with an LLC, you and your business are separate entities and the assets in an LLC can be protected against a lawsuit.

For tax implications, though, there are other options. Let's use an S corporation as an example. This is a different type of legal structure a business can be registered under and it has the benefit of only taxing a portion of the business's money. For example, say you made $100,000 profit for your business in a single year. With an S corporation, you have the ability to only claim a portion of that as income while the other portion comes out as a distribution that doesn't need to pay employment taxes.

UTILIZE TAX ADVANTAGES OF THAT BUSINESS

Once again, the government incentivizes businesses that ⌣ generate more money to be paid into taxes. And there are several key incentives businesses can take advantage of that individuals or employees cannot. Since we love our passive income streams, and rental properties are one area we love to deal in, let's start with the benefits put in place there.

PROPERTY SAVINGS

Do you operate a business from your home? Or do you have office equipment that you need at your house to do your job effectively? These are things that can be written off at tax time if you own a business—something employees are unable to do.

And it goes beyond the simple home and office write-offs. Ever hear of IRS code 280A(g)? This part of the tax code details how any property you own that has a sleeping area, cooking facility, and meeting space could be rented for up to fourteen days per year without having to pay taxes on that income.

Do you have regular team meetings for your office? As long as you use the house for legitimate business purposes, you can bill your company for the time spent at your house for work-related purposes and that income is tax-free. That means your business could pay you for the rental fee, like it would have paid a local venue. And you don't have to report that income. Doing this up to fourteen times throughout the year could save you $10,000 to $25,000 in taxes depending on the size of your house and your tax bracket.

This little piece of IRS code actually began back in the Eisenhower presidency in Augusta, Georgia, when people wanted tax breaks for renting their homes during the Master's tournament, and is oftentimes referred to as the Augusta Rule. But it's still written in the tax code today and can allow you to keep more of the money you earn on those rentals.

BUSINESS WRITE-OFFS

Another way to save money on taxes as a business that you can't do as an individual or employee is to utilize those receipts. Office supplies, business lunches, airline travel—you name it, you keep the receipt for it and turn it in every year.

For the average person, things like a dinner with coworkers or friends isn't a write-off. But for business owners, it can be. And when we say business owner, this can be you and your single-person LLC taking your friends out for a meal. So long as you are discussing the aspects of your business and the dinner has potential to move your business further, you can write off the meal, saving you in taxes at the end of the year.

DEPRECIATION

Let's think small here and then let's move over and think bigger. Starting small, think about your laptop, your printer, your desk, and any other furniture and hardware you need to operate your business. These all have the benefit of being written off as depreciating assets for your business.

What does this mean? It means the US government realizes that the value of assets will go down. Time will have its way with your house, your computer, and all your other physical equipment you need to operate. Nothing lasts forever and since you need these things in great working order to create those jobs—and the subsequent tax revenue—the government is willing to let you write off a little bit of those assets' value each year.

One of the most common, effective write-offs for a business is the use of automobiles, so let's take a work truck as an example. Russ has a $90,000 Range Rover. According to the IRS code section 179, this qualifies as a business asset as long as the business pays for the maintenance and fuel, and it's used for business purposes.

Why else would he let Joey ride in it?

In 2020, the accelerated depreciation rules allowed for these size vehicles to be depreciated 100 percent in that year. That means that Russ's $90,000 Range Rover cost him, after the tax write-off, $54,000.

Sounds great, doesn't it? Now let's think bigger. Let's talk about real estate.

Imagine buying a piece of multifamily real estate for over $1 million. Not only does this property produce thousands of dollars in positive cash flow each month, but it can also create hundreds of thousands of dollars in depreciation write-offs.

Want to know why some of the wealthiest people in our country pay low amounts in taxes? It's because they don't owe a ton of money the way people might think. That's right. Depreciation write-offs allow them to show little to no income each year.

When in Rome, do what the Romans do. In this case, invest in assets that allow you to write off the depreciation.

PAY YOUR CHILDREN

This could change between the time we are writing this and the time you are reading it, but paying your children is another tax-deductible way to keep more of your money. You will want to research the numbers during the year you are reading this, but the US government allows for a standard deduction to be put in place for taxpayers. This means that, up to a certain threshold, no income taxes need to be paid.

Say the standard deduction is $12,000 per year, meaning zero dollars in federal taxes need to be paid on the first $12,000 a taxpayer makes. If this is the case, you can pay your children up to $12,000 per year to do work inside your business, tax-free.

How does this help you? All the money you spend to feed your children, pay for their sports and activities, and for tournaments and hotel rooms can now be paid for out of their account. Your business has expensed the payroll, reducing your taxable income, and they didn't have to pay federal taxes on the money to receive it.

This means that you have more money to buy things you were already paying for. You also get an opportunity to teach your children about personal finance. When they realize that it's their money that is being spent for the art class or new baseball equipment, it will give them a whole different sense of responsibility.

Now, granted, you can't pay your kids $12,000 for one hour of shredding paper—the IRS will catch onto that one pretty quickly—but you can pay your children a reasonable fee to help do work inside your business.

For example, we have both paid our daughters to come onto our podcast and to help us market the business. They travel to conferences with us and get paid to do so. It helps us with the business and it helps them as well.

Many of our clients pay their children to do things like monitoring social media or helping with their online presence. If you have a teenager with a phone, they can be paid to help you. Companies spend tens of thousands of dollars each year to protect their brand integrity and name. But you? You have that teenager who hangs out in their room and stares into their phone all day long. You have the advantage.

TAXES AND IBC

You think we would go into a chapter on taxes without talking about our beloved Infinite Banking? No way. We couldn't do it. This process is too critical to our lives. The framework provides too many benefits not to include it here.

We recommend that people creating passive income consult a tax professional on whether they should incorporate their activities for potential benefits that were previously discussed.

However, paying taxes is inevitable. The tax man will collect whether we like it or not and although there are plenty of ways to lower or limit the amount you will need to dish out, odds are you will have to pay *something*. For some of us, that something might be a little more than we'd like to pay. Especially if we forego paying quarterly payments like the IRS requests and instead, pay annually. When this happens, the lump sum can be quite large. Add on the roughly 2 percent charge the IRS tacks on to that for paying annually instead of quarterly and you've got yourself a number with a few zeros on the end.

Most of us don't keep that much cash lying around the house. We invest it. We buy assets that generate cash flow and then we put that cash flow back into additional investment paths. We're not in the business of saving because sitting on a whole bunch of cash means being in a losing battle with inflation.

So we invest. We keep our money in motion, buying new assets, creating more cash flow that buys even more assets, which creates even more cash flow.

If this is the case, and you operate in this function, how is it that you can have enough cash on hand to pay that large tax bill every year?

IBC is how.

With Infinite Banking and a whole life policy, your policy—

or your system of policies—becomes the reservoir that you use to save and pay your taxes each year. This allows your money to always be growing and make it more efficient. All you need to do is make a quick phone call or click a couple buttons online and you have money to turn over to the government—no prison time for not paying taxes.

The best part? Once you borrow against your IBC system, you now have a place to store those tax payments. This process reduces your insurance loan and will provide the holding account for the next year's tax bill.

Oh yeah, and the money in there? It grows tax-free.

Have we mentioned how much we love Infinite Banking?

HAVE CONTROL

Picture yourself seated at a table getting ready to sign papers for a new home you're about to buy. You have your pen handy and you're ready to sign on the (many, many) dotted lines. You go through page after page, seeing various numbers and trying to make sure each one of them makes sense.

Purchase price, loan amount, property taxes, title costs, monthly payment—there's so much to go through, but it's all there, clearly calculated and written down. You flip the page once more and on that page, you see the finance terms. There's a line for the interest rate and it reads: *TBD—To Be Determined.*

You freeze. *I'm sorry, what? What's going on here?*

Are you going to sign those papers? Will you take on a thirty-year mortgage when you have no idea what the interest rate is going to be for the next thirty years? Heck, would you take on *any* loan when you don't know what the interest rate will be for just *one* year?

You wouldn't, would you? Of course not. So why would

you sign up to put your money into all these stock-market-dependent retirement Plans that tell you taxes won't need to be paid until you cash out? Do you have any idea what the tax rate will be when you're in your sixties?

There's no control in that scenario. You're at the mercy of, *one*, whatever the stock market does over the course of your time working, and *two*, whatever the politicians in Washington say the tax rate will be in the year you're eligible to start taking back some of that money you've invested.

STEP THREE

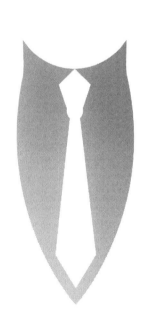

FIND A
SUPPORT
SYSTEM OF
LIKE-MINDED
INDIVIDUALS

CHAPTER EIGHT

INVESTOR DNA

"Not only that, but we rejoice in our sufferings, knowing that suffering produces endurance, and endurance produces character, and character produces hope."

—ROMANS 5:3–4

While you're on your path to Financial Freedom through passive income, there is a lot of advice to be retained. There's a ton to learn and to absorb, whether it be through our community or through the many others available today. But there's a bit of a problem with all of the messaging. There's a whole lot of information about *where* you are on your journey and what you can do about it, but there isn't much about *who* you are and why that matters.

The frameworks introduced so far in this book can tell you where you are. They give you insight on how to judge yourself and your financial decisions in life, open your mind to new and unique ways to create passive income, and even give you some insight on how to capitalize by structuring a business.

All are great things to learn and having more options is

certainly better than none, but the whole point of going down this path toward Financial Freedom is to live a happier life. The point is to allow you to enjoy the things that you do and make money in the process. So charting the wrong course toward that desired end goal could turn out to be just another set of frustrating tasks for you, and that's the last thing you want to do.

What if you start investing in something and realize that you weren't a great fit for the investment? How much precious time could be lost in that process?

What you need to know is *who* you are, because who you are applies to building passive income. What are the types of things that interest you? What are the gifts that you were given at birth and talents that you have acquired through life that could be used toward your freedom journey? Connecting with what you are investing in not only produces greater results but greater happiness.

You want passive income so that you can create happiness. So that you can serve a purpose and complete the mission that God put you on this earth to do. That's why it is important to choose the paths that align with your personality and pursue a framework that focuses on those paths.

To do so, you need to dive deep into your personality traits—your Investor DNA. A personality assessment is the best way to discover these.

PERSONALITY ASSESSMENT RESULTS

When clients first come to us for guidance on how to create freedom through passive income, they are typically a little antsy to get going. And who wouldn't be? Who wouldn't want to start moving the needle as quickly as possible? But one of the primary steps we take with each of these clients is to determine the investments best suited for their personality and their agenda.

Joey has a prime example of this. In the midst of the drop-shipping craze, he was presented with a promising website: 100unicorns.com. It fell far outside of the investments he was used to but the opportunity presented itself during an ideal time. He jumped in, hoping it would work out.

It didn't. Not only was Joey unfamiliar with the business, but he wasn't in love with the idea. A website that sells unicorn clothing? It was a great business for his daughters, but not for Joey. It turned out to be a disaster and has cost more money than it earned.

Had Joey been passionate about the industry, he would have gone out of his way to ensure he scaled the business. But he wasn't.

We don't want to see you make the same mistakes. Think about which industries you want to be a part of. If you don't know off the top of your head, start doing some research into possibilities.

There are personality assessments all over the internet that can help you to discover more about your interests. There are none—that we know of—that match you with investment opportunities. So we decided we would create one, taking the way individuals see the world and how they will view different opportunities.

We tested this concept and found that there are generally four different personality types.

FIRST:

The first is the straightforward individual. The person who is results-oriented and wants things done quickly. For a business-person, this is someone with a focus on their bottom line who sees the future and can make sure things are done that will help improve that number.

For investing, this person usually likes to get into areas with proven results, or proven return on investment (ROI), because they want things done with speed. Getting things done supersedes any sort of emotion behind their decisions. Facts and numbers tell the story here and those are the results they want.

SECOND:

The second type of personality is the individual who prides themself on being personable. They are charismatic and get things done on a more personal level. They tend to learn by experiencing things compared to reading about them. The bottom line and checking off their task list isn't always a top priority. Instead, bringing people together and working in a collaborative manner drives them.

Income streams for this type of person usually lie in collaborations. You could say the two of us fall into this category since we are collaborating on this book, but let's not jump to conclusions just yet. We still have two more personality types to go.

THIRD:

The third personality type is one that isn't as outspoken as the second, nor as aggressive as the first. Instead, they tend to rely a little more on their inner thoughts. They want things done right rather than done quickly and if it takes a little while longer to accomplish their overall goals, then so be it.

Investments for this personality type don't need to have quick ROI, they just need to be stable. Proven. There can be some wiggle room for risk but for the most part, they would rather trade a little bit of their time in return for working on a framework that they know will be profitable.

FOURTH:

The final of the four personality types is the person who likes to play it safe. They seek logic before making any sort of decision and would prefer not to take any big gambles the way a person in the first assessment class would do.

Their investment portfolio could resemble that of someone in the third category where they want options that are safe and secure. Even if they don't produce the possibility of a massive gain, a person sitting in this category is more than happy seeing small yet guaranteed gains.

This person enjoys following a process and loves businesses and activities that allow systems to produce returns.

PASSIVE INCOME MATRIX

Now that you know which category your personality falls within, we're going to introduce you to the Passive Income, or PI, Matrix. What this PI Matrix is going to do is allow you to narrow down even further which investment paths are right for you.

The PI Matrix is a series of charts that will display the pros, cons, and key factors of each of your possible investment paths in proportion to each of the four types of Investor DNA. By using these charts, you can easily identify not only which investment paths would work best for you and your situation, but you can know *why*.

More importantly, you can begin to take into account these pros and cons to formulate a list of your top investment paths. This is important, especially for those type A personalities that feel as though they can take on *every* investment path. Surely, it won't be possible to do them all—not at the onset of your financial journey, anyway. So these matrices will help you to get going with ones that best fit your personality and needs, and that you will enjoy taking part in.

The Pros Matrix is the one that can get you the most motivated, especially at the beginning. While looking through the pros of each, it's easy to get caught up in the excitement. That's why we created the Cons Matrix.

The Cons Matrix is what will ground you. It will open your eyes to some of the negatives of specific investments that may steer you away, based on your personality. That being said, cons for one personality type might not necessarily be cons for another, which is why they are broken into these sections.

And finally, there's the Key Factors Matrix, which indicates some of the most necessary things to operate each possible investment path. This matrix gives you a glimpse into what will be required of you and your resources. Is your time already consumed by your full-time job and other responsibilities? Is capital critical? Will great detail be required? These are all things the Key Factors Matrix will reveal.

A member of our community used this Passive Income Matrix for himself when the COVID-19 pandemic forced him to find new ways to earn an income. As a commissioned sales representative, the pandemic closed his sales pipeline immediately and he needed help. He didn't jump into the first path he came across. Instead, he joined our IBC community after being referred by a friend, did his research, and then decided on his best option. Now, he's doing well with his choice. More importantly, he's happy in what he's doing.

> Study the matrix for yourself and determine what it is that you would like to do. With your Investment DNA in place and the PI Matrix available to give you a glimpse into the requirements of each option, it's now time to move forward with your choice(s).
>
> www.wealthwithoutwallstreet.com/book

CHOOSING YOUR FRAMEWORK

Of course, there aren't hard lines drawn in the sand with these four categories or within the PI Matrix. We are all unique, and a blend of two or even three of these isn't out of the question. So if you find yourself relating to more than one of these, that's perfectly normal. In fact, it may even be helpful, because it opens up a few more options for income streams that you may find interesting.

And who knows? Partnerships may even arise from this matrix. This assessment isn't meant to deter you from pursuing certain strategies altogether. In some cases, it just requires a partnership with others. The values of partnerships become so much clearer after doing the assessment. This is something Joey can admit to doing with short-term rentals. He was skeptical about the path but Russ was so adamant about pursuing it that Joey caved and went with it. That turned out to be a good choice that only happened because of a partnership.

The PI Matrix is meant to open your eyes. Once you have an idea of the types of processes you would like to be a part of, your options start to become clearer. Sure, you have an abundance of terms to choose from when it comes to passive income sources, but knowing your personality type and how each of those plays into your strengths pulls some of them to the top of the list. Then, with a narrow base to choose from, you can begin to realize which you want to learn more about and which you want to subsequently pursue.

From there, it's a matter of the time and energy you want to put into these passive income sources. Do you want a hands-on opportunity or would you prefer to be hands-off? Your time commitment matters just as much as your choice of investment.

Chapters Nine and Ten will cover both the hands-on and hands-off approaches in more depth, but it's important to look into the preliminary things before deciding which of these you want to choose. Otherwise, obstacles will certainly be waiting for you.

You'll get to where you want to go either way. If you are reading this book and investing your time into improving your financial life and your financial future, there's no doubt that you will eventually reach a point of Financial Freedom. Hands-on or hands-off approach won't matter. But if you pick one you enjoy, the ride from A to B will be smooth and, more importantly, it will be fun.

Choosing the wrong path can be discouraging and that's what happens to a lot of people who simply find themselves in careers and life courses they don't like. The two of us are prime examples, one financial planner and one mortgage loan originator, both making great money but spending all of our time inside of our jobs rather than doing what we wanted to be doing.

Money isn't everything. Happiness is. So find the investment path that makes you happiest and begin putting a framework around it.

WHERE TO ASSESS YOURSELF

Have some ideas about which cash-flowing strategies you want to pursue? Great. That's a fantastic start. Validating those emotions with more objective data is the next step.

Before making any moves, head on over to our website and take the online assessment. By taking a few minutes up front to get an idea of your true, inner personality, you can avoid a lot of headache in the future.

www.wealthwithoutwallstreet.com/book

CHAPTER NINE

ZERO CAPITAL DOESN'T MEAN ZERO OPTIONS

"One who is faithful in a very little is also faithful in much, and one who is dishonest in a very little is also dishonest in much."

—LUKE 16:10

Before we move into your options for investing, let's talk about the one thing that seems to hold people back from getting started. It's the main barrier to entering a life of Financial Freedom: the belief that you need to have money to make money.

But not everybody starts out with money. Some, like us, needed to start small and get creative along the way.

Some people call their free labor at the beginning of a new venture *sweat equity*. Others call it a *five-to-nine* or a *side hustle*. You use whichever terminology you desire because at the end of the day, it all means the same thing: sacrificing your time now so that you can live a simpler life later.

Here's a stat you might like to read: four in five American millionaires are first generation, self-made. That means they didn't inherit any of their wealth, they earned it. They did so by sacrificing their time at the beginning for that big payout at the end.

Want that to be you? It can be, but you need to put in some work at the beginning. Make it a side hustle. Keep that full-time job so your family can depend on you and work on your passive income streams in addition to that job. It might be this way for a few months, or even a few years, but this is your starting point. Committing to making this side hustle a real, tangible thing is the first thing you can do in order to get going.

ROBERTO CHAVEZ

After seven-plus years of working as an attorney, I was sitting in my office overlooking downtown, and my heart was racing with my letter of resignation in my hands. I felt a mix of emotions as I prepared to walk over to my boss's office and let him know that I was going to be leaving my legal career behind to pursue my land business full time.

This journey started three and a half years prior to that moment. I had been listening to podcasts and reading books about how people were generating other forms of income and creating a life on their terms. I had created a substantial debt while in college and even though the income I was receiving from my legal practice was good, it wasn't making that much of a difference. I still felt behind.

As I envisioned what my life would look like in ten to fifteen years if I did not do anything differently, I realized that I could be making good money at the law firm, but it was going to be an **exchange for my time**. I did not like what I saw and knew I needed to find a way out.

I do not know if it was destiny or what, but I bumped into this podcast with this geeky guy, Mark Podolsky (a.k.a. the Land Geek), who flips land. The more I heard the business model, the more it made sense, and the more I knew it was something that I could do.

This business model showed me that I could do something once (sell a piece of property) and get income from it for the next five to ten years. That was mind blowing! At the same time, it was frustrating that I had not heard of this before. If there were people out there doing this, why couldn't I do it?

This new opportunity fueled me to learn the business, get coaching in the business, and work the business after hours and on weekends. It took me a little over two years to replace my legal practice income with selling land on monthly terms. The last one and a half years before I quit my job, I spent developing a mindset that I did not have to depend on a check from my work every two weeks. That was the hard part.

Life looks differently now; I no longer trade my time for money. Life is rich.

Your next steps should be to choose from the options you are about to read and select one or two that you can see yourself being fully committed to. Learn the aspects of those businesses inside and out and work within them to get things off the ground. As you begin to make more money, you can then spend some of that money to hire others to take over your workload—consultants, property managers, virtual assistants, and so forth.

Charting your passive income course is no different than a business owner forming their company. Take any big-name CEO or business owner and look at their path. Mark Zuckerberg, Jeff Bezos, any of them. They all began their projects by doing everything on their own, and then they were able to grow to a size that they had others who could do the work for them while they continued to collect money.

Now look at what happens in their business. They can take off for months at a time and it will continue to operate effectively. Why is that? Because they put in all the work up front to ensure the systems and processes were in place. They took all their time to find the best methods and the most efficient processes and they designed them in a system that can be utilized by anybody they put into their place.

In Robert Kiyosaki's book *Rich Dad's Cashflow Quadrant*, he introduces the four quadrants people fit into. The left side of the quadrant holds the letters E and S—E for employee and S for self-employed. In these two roles, a person cannot take off for months at a time without severe damage to their financial situation. Money doesn't flow unless they trade their time in exchange.

On the right side of the quadrant are the letters B and I—B for business owner and I for investor. Those in these roles can take off for months at a time and money will not become a factor. They have built passive income processes that allow them to have Financial Freedom.

The right side of that quadrant is where you want to be. But you can't jump into those quadrants right away. Some hands-on work may need to be done beforehand.

CREATIVE FINANCING

If you're thinking to yourself, *Joey and Russ, getting my hands dirty and working my butt off to get where I need to be sounds great and all, but where do I get the funding cash to get going?* then you should listen to what we're about to tell you regarding OPM, or other people's money.

People have been misinformed into thinking that having their own money is the only way to get started in business, in investing, or any other cash flow initiative. Or that going to a traditional bank and asking for a high-interest loan is another. But neither of those is true. They're both options, of course, but they aren't the only ones. Far from it.

Using OPM is quite common, even for the rich who have their own money. It's actually more likely for a truly wealthy person to use someone else's money to do a deal than it is for them to use theirs.

Private money and using OPM are beneficial because the terms in these creatively financed deals are often much better than what you could find traditionally. Plus, they can be agreed upon and funds can be transferred much quicker than banks are able to do.

There are so many ways to creatively finance your endeavors. Below are some of the common terms you will hear.

SELLER FINANCING

Looking to get into real estate but don't have the cash on hand? With a major tax benefit like depreciation on your side, it's no wonder you like this investment path so much. But real estate deals can be daunting. They can take forever to get to the finish line.

With seller financing, the current owner—the seller—of the house becomes the bank. This is great for those who want to get into real estate investing but may not have some of the prerequisites mortgage lenders require.

Seller financing means you may have to pay the seller a down payment and then the subsequent monthly payments thereafter. You agree upon your own terms and as long as you make your payments on time, the home is yours—same as your deal with a bank.

Oftentimes, sellers like this option because they can earn passive income at a higher rate than what might be available to them if they instead had been paid off at the purchase date, forced to find somewhere else to invest that large sum of money. Not to mention, they understand that if you fail to pay them, the house becomes theirs and they get to do it all over again. Nothing is lost.

HARD MONEY

Hard money loans are, again, mostly used in real estate. These are good creative financing paths for home- or land-flippers who see the potential to make money quickly.

Hard money lenders—think bookies for real estate—don't care about your credit score, your payment history, or even your current income. All they want to see is the purchase price you can get the property for *now* versus what you can sell it for, it's after repair value (ARV). If you can prove to a hard money lender that the numbers are accurate and that the potential to make money is almost guaranteed, the money to get started is yours. The benefits to these types of loans are there is very little money required as a down payment and the payments are interest only.

Be careful, though, because hard money loans can come with higher interest rates. Since they are designed to be short-term loans, it's typically not a big deal to sign on at a high rate. However, if the house doesn't sell and you need to start paying back that loan, it could leave your wallet holding nothing but air.

CASH-OUT REFINANCE

Whether it's your primary residence or another property you own, a cash-out refinance might be an alternative to free up access to cash. A cash-out refinance is a model to restructure your existing loan and take out the current equity in the home.

Cash-out refinances have changed over the years. When Joey was in the mortgage industry, lenders would go up to 95 percent loan-to-value (LTV) on these types of refinances. But banks are limiting their risks more and more, now capping LTV at 80 percent at the time we write this book.

Here's how a cash-out refinance works. Say you bought your home for $200,000 but you have paid off $50,000 since you moved in. This would mean you have $50,000 worth of equity in your home. Now add the fact that housing prices have gone up 15 percent, bringing your home's value to $230,000. Between the housing price increase of $30,000 (the increase in home value of $230,000 minus the initial purchase cost of $200,000) plus the $50,000 principal reduction of your mortgage, you have $80,000 worth of equity in your home.

If the bank's cash-out refinance limits are 80 percent LTV, then you would have the ability to get $34,000 in cash.

Current Home Value	$230,000
Current LTV Ratio of 80 Percent	× 80% [$184,000]
Principal Remaining on the Mortgage	− $150,000
	= $34,000

Having this cash on hand allows you to purchase more cash-flowing opportunities. Many long-term real estate investors utilize this method to come up with the cash for the down payment on another purchase.

HELOC

A HELOC, or home equity line of credit, works similarly to a cash-out refinance. If you have equity in your home, you can pull out the cash to use.

A HELOC is different in that it doesn't provide you with all the money up front, at once, the way a cash-out refinance does. Instead, you have access to a line of credit that is backed by your home's equity. Think of it like a credit card with your home equity being the collateral.

You can tap into those funds as needed and only pay interest on what you take. LTV caps also go a bit higher, as high as 90 percent for this type of credit.

TAP INTO THAT RETIREMENT FUND

It might seem like we despise Wall Street, and we really do, but maybe for a different reason than you think. It's not the fact that stocks, bonds, and mutual funds are risky and the majority of people who invest in them have absolutely no way to influence the outcome—which they don't. It's that when they are invested in Wall Street, it's often within a qualified retirement plan that locks away their money and prevents them from starting their Financial Freedom journey today.

These types of accounts also determine when it is that you are able to retire. Any time before 59 ½ years old and you're penalized for withdrawing your own money? How does that make sense? This is just another way to keep you working for someone else while Wall Street makes money off of your money. And we simply know from firsthand experience that there are much better options available.

However, if you have retirement accounts, you have slowly been building them. And although Wall Street uses those funds to make money for themselves, you maybe can still access it. There will most likely be penalties but if you need the money and can afford to pay the fees to get your own money back, this is an option. You can then put that money into investments over which you have more control.

USE YOUR WHOLE LIFE POLICY

Have we mentioned IBC with a whole life policy yet? It's actually been a bit too long since we *have* mentioned it, but having the ability to simply pick up the phone and initiate a loan is one of the greatest perks of IBC. No credit checks. No approval needed. You are in complete control.

And remember, if you borrow $20,000 against your policy as a policy loan with a $50,000 cash value, that $20,000 is still counted toward the total balance of your account. That means it continues to grow and earn you dividends even though you are using the money to fund your next venture. *You never have to give up the compounding interest of those funds.*

OPTIONS ARE CONSTANTLY EVOLVING

This list isn't finite. If you become creative, you can find other ways to finance your efforts. Maybe a family member or friend has come into money and is looking to invest it. Or a new method of lending opens its doors to the public and you find it valuable.

CHAPTER TEN

HANDS-ON OPTIONS

"The soul of the sluggard craves and gets nothing, while the soul of the diligent is richly supplied."

—PROVERBS 13:4

Wait a second, Russ and Joey. Isn't this book about Financial Freedom through passive investments? Why are we even talking about hands-on approaches to gaining cash flow?

Well, that depends. How did your assessment come back? What were the results? Did the assessment reveal that you like safer investments or that you prefer to take risks? The results of the assessment described in the previous chapter will help you to map out your course. It will help you to decide which path, or paths, to take.

But there's another significant factor at play when you're getting ready to begin your journey and that's the money you have at the onset. As the old adage goes, you need money to make money. And although it is possible to make that initial money in order to let your investments take off, a little bit of legwork will be required at the beginning.

The truth of the matter is that passive income doesn't always mean kicking back and watching the checks roll in. As J. Massey said, "Passive income doesn't mean being uninvolved." Plus, most people don't have the up-front capital to make that kind of lifestyle work—the beach-going lifestyle that the retirement lie (more on that in the final chapter) continues to show us. Sometimes passive income has to start as a side hustle.

So what do we need to do first? We need to get our hands a little dirty. Rather than handing over a lump sum of money to a manager and having them do everything for us, we need to learn a little bit. Be involved in the day-to-day activities of the investment path with which we are about to partake.

This doesn't always mean swinging a hammer and becoming an electrician if, for example, you're getting into real estate. It just means being a part of the operation. Understanding. Learning. Taking your progress each day and applying it toward that overall goal of being able to have hands-off investments.

There are four things needed to make deals happen and to create passive income: money, experience, time, and the deal itself. Thankfully, you don't need to provide all four. Time and experience will allow you to learn the others as you go.

Okay, ready to get started? The options below are some of the most common hands-on approaches to investing. Again, all investing options—even those hands-off options listed in the next chapter—begin as hands-on, but these are the ones that tend to remain hands-on throughout the duration of the time they are producing cash flow.

LONG-TERM RENTALS

Long-term property rentals are what most people picture when they hear the term *real estate investor*. They think of the person having multiple single-family homes for rent, or a landlord renting out apartments to tenants. Either way, the month-to-month basis is what people think of.

There are five ways to make money in buying and owning rental properties: *positive cash flow*, *equity capture* (acquiring the property below market value), *appreciation* (an increase in price), *depreciation* (tax advantages that we discussed earlier), and *mortgage balance reduction* (renters paying down the mortgage).

While cash flow may be the most talked about benefit of long-term rentals, the other four provide some incredible value. Just think about what you can do with all five of these working together. Do you see why we choose to put our money into assets instead of paying down debts?

SHORT-TERM RENTALS

Short-term rental properties have been a booming business since mobile apps have become popular and we have entered a new "shared economy." These are the places listed on Vrbo and Airbnb. They are short-term vacation rentals or nightly stays in fully furnished apartments, houses, condos, and rooms. But they also include boats, Airstreams, RVs, and believe it or not, tree houses.

The short-term rental (STR) business is a hospitality business. You can choose to own the real estate or you can lease it from someone else. The latter is oftentimes referred to as the "arbitrage" model. It allows you to rent on a long-term basis from the owner and make the difference between what you earn on a monthly basis renting it short-term versus your monthly rent.

As a STR host, you are responsible for the utilities, cleaning, supplies, and furnishing the palace. This process, though, can be more cash flow lucrative than long-term rentals. In our experience, we have found short-term rentals tend to profit closer to $500 per bedroom as compared to $150 per bedroom for equivalent long-term rental units.

We started our STR business with one unit in July of 2020 and grew it to over twenty-five units in only eighteen months. Explaining the process for this could turn into a book on its own so we'll leave it at that for now. If you are interested in learning more about this business, go to our reference page link.

www.wealthwithoutwallstreet.com/book

LAND-FLIPPING

Struggling to find startup cash? Land-flipping can be an option with one of the lower barriers to entry to start making cash flow. All you have to do is find cheap land—and in some parts of the country, you can find land for under $100—and then turn around and resell it for a higher price.

This is something we have also done on our own, growing the business over the past twelve months to over $10,000 per month in *positive cash flow*. Like STR, there's much more detail to this than could fit into this section of the book.

To learn more about this option, use the link to our Resources page where you will find a webinar walking you through the steps to get started.

E-COMMERCE

An e-commerce business can be a few different things, but what it means in a broad sense is that you buy and sell things online.

Just as land-flipping is a business of buying low and selling for a higher price, so too is e-commerce.

If you can find a way to make money from e-commerce, not only can you capitalize on a growing trend, but you can do so from essentially anywhere in the world.

Be careful not to confuse this with drop-shipping or arbitrage, though. These are things that people online will tout as moneymakers, but the online marketplace has continued to crack down on these practices.

The true path to e-commerce success is to create your own white-label products. Build them and sell on a legitimate marketplace like Amazon. A member of our Inner Circle found success doing exactly this. As a full-time pastor, he was looking for ways to add income when he came upon our podcast promoting this idea of selling white-label products on Amazon. Soon after, he was making several thousand dollars per month in extra income.

If you want to hear more about this story and how it unfolded, listen to our podcast episode #183. Again, there's simply too much information to include here. If we went into detail with each of these processes, this book would be another hundred pages and it would be all over the place.

BUILD SYSTEMS THAT RUN THEMSELVES

We talked in Chapter Seven about the tax advantages of being your own business, but let's face it: a lot of us have jobs. We have things we need to do on a daily basis that require us to trade time for money. We all have little free time remaining because of this, which is why this Hands-on Options chapter might not have appealed to you. Even if it did, there are only so many hours you could spend with your hands inside other income sources.

If you enjoy your full-time position and you simply want to create some passive income to bring in extra money, great. Building a side hustle over time as a five-to-nine might be the perfect method for you. If you build the right systems and hire people to replace you, you can eventually fade out of the day-to-day.

For those who dislike their full-time occupations, however, and are starting this as a means to escape the nightmare they have to drive into every day, know that this will take time. Again, it is a process. A framework. And it needs to be built as such. Just like a house isn't built in a day, neither is a new passive income stream with little up-front capital.

The overall goal is to build systems that run themselves, which is like building a house that can stand on its own. Sure, if you're up and at it, building all day every day, the house will be finished sooner. But if your time is limited and this framework is only being built while burning the midnight oil, it will take longer.

That's okay. Be patient. It will all come together eventually. And before you know it, all the hard work will pay off in the form of approaches that require much less effort on your part: the hands-off approaches.

Confused about where to begin or need a little boost off the starting line? Helping to design a framework for our clients and our community is one of the things we do most often. If you're ready to go through coaching and have the desire to truly educate yourself on the field you are about to enter, a little guidance may be just what you need.

If this sounds like you, head on over to www.wealth withoutwallstreet.com/book and schedule a free consultation call with one of our trusted coaches.

CHAPTER ELEVEN

HANDS-OFF APPROACH

"Wealth gained hastily will dwindle, but whoever gathers little by little will increase it."

—PROVERBS 13:11

As we move away from the Hands-on Options chapter and into guidance on hands-off income streams, it's important to note one thing:

We recommend that all investment activities are hands-on at the beginning.

We want to make this clear because there are a lot of people who hear the term *hands-off* and think, *Oh, I can hand this off to someone else* or *I don't have the time for this so let me just hire somebody.*

The easy-button approach to handing something off to an "expert" has gotten you here. Is *here* where you want to be? I mean, are you financially free where your **PI > ME**? If the answer is no, then tread lightly into this section. Don't get sucked into delegating your freedom into the hands of someone else.

Hands-off by way of hiring others to do your investing for

you *is* a thing, but it's only for those who have a ton of wealth and want to simply put their money to work elsewhere. Remember, there are four ways to get into deals that can create passive income: cash, experience, time, and the deal itself. These will get the needle moving on your investments. And our Passive Income MasterMind on our Resources page will give you all the details and the Support group you need to get going.

Don't overlook that second one—the Support group. Being in a group with people both above and below you can be a great experience. If you need a boost, people are always there, ready to help push each other. It's an incredible atmosphere that will help get you on the right path toward a specific framework.

Once you have created a framework that can, for the most part, operate itself, hands-off becomes possible. And that dream of having Financial Freedom through passive income becomes something that's no longer a dream, but is close to becoming reality.

THE TRANSITION

Young people have energy. We know because we used to be there. But as we get older, those energy sources get harder to come by. This is why we strive to set up a framework that allows for less hands-on work as we get older and begin to put our money to work for us instead of us going to work for our money.

When the time is right to transition from an energy-dependent system to one that gives you more time-flexibility and -freedom, you can feel confident knowing that you have done everything you can to put the proper processes in place.

Learning the business and understanding its needs allows you to hire the right people to replace you. As one of our clients said to us, "I want to work hard for eighteen months so that I can buy back the forty hours a week I would have to put in for the rest of my life." This client was building his land-flipping business to a point that the monthly note income would replace his day job.

You can do this too. And when more time opens up, you can look into options that are more hands-off from the start. Although, as a disclaimer here again, very few things are 100 percent hands-off. The options below, however, will be much less time consuming than the ones listed above.

HANDS-OFF OPTIONS

Experience with hands-on techniques will teach you everything you need to know. But time will become an issue. You won't be able to remain hands-on as you continue to grow your assets and investments. At some point, you will need to move out of the day-to-day and allow others to take the wheel.

When you've hit this point, here are some options investors tend to turn to when they want to remain hands-off.

TURNKEY PROPERTIES

For investors who have little time and are willing to trade money for a deal that can quickly start cash-flowing, turnkey properties can be great options. The term is sometimes used vaguely and it won't always be that all turnkey properties are the same. But for the most part, they are homes that have been recently renovated to lower short-term maintenance needs. Many of these turnkey properties also find the renter for you *and* manage the tenant monthly.

Some areas to consider when working with turnkey providers is the demographics within the city where the homes are being bought. Is the city growing in population? Finding and buying homes in growing cities can prove to be much safer and more lucrative than doing so in a city with a declining population.

Other things to look into are the average vacancy of the providers and how many evictions they have had in the last twelve months. Both of these can give you an idea of the rental market and how diligent the screening process is that's conducted by the turnkey provider.

PRIVATE LENDING

Many of our clients who have set up their IBC systems have taken the idea of becoming a bank literally. Becoming a private lender can allow you to invest in everything we have talked about so far without having to take on the risks of each of those businesses.

Banks lend money to people who put up a good chunk of money as a down payment but need to finance the rest. They do this only for those who have demonstrated an expertise in the area for which they are borrowing money. And as your own bank, you can do this as well.

If you don't have interest in taking on the risk of investing in real estate, private lending is an option for bringing in cash flow that's completely hands-off. As a private lender, you can loan money to borrowers for a variety of things—property, land, auto, business. If you're lending your own money, the choice is up to you.

Since you're loaning out your own money, you also get to dictate terms and interest rates. You can also choose the loans you are willing to hand out. For us, loans with significant collateral are the only route we like to take, and we suggest the same for anyone looking to get into lending.

There are simple ways to get into private lending now, including peer-to-peer lending sites. You can choose the level of risk you want to take with regard to borrowers and the amount you, yourself, are willing to risk.

Hard money loans, which were discussed in the Creative Financing portion of Chapter Nine, can also be an option for you. Unlike in Chapter Nine when you were on the borrowing side of the deal, you can now be on the lending end. Potential borrowers will come to you with distressed homes, plans for repairing such homes, and the potential profits when sold. All you do is write the check and then wait for the payments to come in. Not a bad deal if you land some homes with significant profit potential.

It also works well for the person borrowing the money from you. Traditional banks have so many roadblocks, and for people in fast-moving industries, getting a traditional loan could take too long.

Take house flippers, for example. If a distressed home is being sold at a great price but the person doesn't have cash on hand, there's no way a bank would approve the loan in time to make the purchase. You, as the banker, can get this person access to cash faster.

The two of us offered private lending to a person in a similar situation recently. As collateral on the loan, the guy put up his car—a Chevy Suburban. We ended up making 26 percent on the deal and the guy was able to get the quick funding he needed. It was a win–win. It was such a good process that he actually came back to us again for another loan.

INVEST IN BUSINESSES

No, we're not talking about investing in the stock market. We're talking about investing in small, private companies that allow you to generate cash flow. And it's this final part that's important to note when it comes to investing in businesses.

There's a term, angel investor, that we like to stay away from. An angel investor is a person who gives money to a company in its earliest stages. In exchange, that angel investor receives a decent percentage of ownership in the company. The goal for an angel investor is to buy into a company early, give it time to grow, and then cash out for a large payday.

Sometimes that works, but sometimes it doesn't. Angel investors commonly lose their money if a business they have invested in fails.

We're not talking about angel investing. What we mean when we say invest in businesses is to invest in businesses that are already turning a profit. Instead of buying into a company at its earliest stages, you can invest in a company that simply needs money to expand. Maybe they want to branch into new avenues or expand their current store. Whatever the case, they need money and they are willing to pay you in the form of dividends.

We recently invested in a local candle company that wanted to expand its product line. The primary owner needed capital for this expansion and we offered it to him. In return, we now have equity in the company and we participate in quarterly distribution projections.

Without those distributions, we wouldn't have invested in the business because it wouldn't have offered cash flow. And when it comes to **PI > ME**, cash flow is the key to growing that PI side of the equation.

ATMS

Automatic teller machines, or ATMs, can be another great hands-off passive income opportunity. We all have familiarity with ATMs, don't we?

At some point, you have used an ATM to get some cash. Maybe it was to get some food at a hot dog stand late at night, or when the cash in your wallet disappeared onto the other side of a casino table. Okay, that sounds a little more like us in our twenties but you understand. ATMs have cash and when people need it, they make their way to the machine.

ATMs are placed in areas where people need cash. Although electronic transactions are becoming more common, there is still a large segment of the population that continues to depend on these machines.

The hands-off way to owning ATMs and not having to carry a pistol and large sacks of cash around to refill them is through *syndicate funds*. These funds negotiate leases with the property owners, manage the software updates, and pay armored trucks to deal with the cash. As an owner/investor in these funds, you get to take part in the profit pool—and, as an added bonus, the depreciation of the units themselves.

As with turnkey properties, you will want to look deep into the experience of the manager's fund. But if you find a good manager, this can provide a good source of cash flow.

Personally, we invest in a fund that has seven ATMs in it. We do no maintenance or supplying of cash and they pay us, as investors, a monthly amount for seven years.

Curious as to how this works in more detail or want to see some numbers? Our Passive Income Report can tell you more, breaking down numbers and details. You can find the link to the report on our resources page at www. wealthwithoutwallstreet.com/book.

CRYPTOCURRENCY MINING

Cryptocurrencies have been becoming more and more popular, and although many people are investing in the coins themselves, another viable option is available: mining the coins.

Transactions that take place on a cryptocurrency's "block-chain"—the ledger that houses all the information for each transaction—require verification. There are different techniques for doing the verification but the most popular and effective is called *proof of work* and it is performed by miners. That process pays "miners" a fee, and that fee comes in the form of a crypto coin.

That's an oversimplified version of the process, of course, but it gives you a brief explanation of what happens.

The computers used in mining are specialized, high-performance systems and consume fairly large amounts of energy. Most of these miners across the world are large groups that have been able to negotiate electricity rates significantly lower than what we pay at our homes. Hence, buying one of these computer rigs and plugging it into your spare bedroom is probably not a profitable venture. Your electricity bill would be pretty high from the power running consistently—not to mention the heat produced from the computers, pushing heat into the room and throughout the house.

If you have the space and some technical aptitude, you can look through the benefits to see if this could be something of interest. Not only do you get paid in cryptocurrency for doing the mining, but you earn more as the value of the cryptocurrency rises.

The process takes quite a bit of startup capital since there's a decent amount of hardware involved, but you can have computers running automatically for you, all day and all night, "mining" these coins that are available online. With new coins being popularized almost daily, this is something that will continue to grow in popularity.

KNOW THE PERSONALITY REQUIREMENTS

Don't forget about the personality assessment and what it can tell you about the paths you choose. Your assessment can help you understand if you are about to enter something you enjoy doing or whether you're simply replacing the things you currently dread with something else that you dread.

The personality requirements of both hands-on and hands-off options will vary and the level of time and energy you will need to put into them will also. Before jumping in, take your time. Analyze the implications and think about whether or not you're really ready to take on another task.

Once you weigh your options and choose the right path, your life can change for the better. No longer will you need to rely on the options advertised to us—those Wall-Street-centric options that take your money and allow others to profit off it.

When you set your own course, you remain in control. And that's the entire message behind what we do here at Wealth Without Wall Street.

CHAPTER TWELVE

WEALTH WITHOUT WALL STREET

"Whatever your hand finds to do, do it with your might."
—Ecclesiastes 9:10

Twelve percent. Is that number ringing a bell? If you've been hanging around on Wall Street, it would. Twelve percent represents the annual growth rate we have been told to expect each year we invest in their options—stocks, mutual funds, and so forth. That number is as guaranteed as death and taxes by some Wall Street pundits.

Let's talk about this number—and others—we keep hearing about, shall we? When we hear these assumed historical averages, we make decisions into the future based off of them. We let these numbers cloud the truth and we make decisions that may not be in our best interest.

What if the averages were misleading? What if we didn't receive a 12 percent return and our annual savings weren't enough to allow us to "retire" when we wanted to because of it?

Let's do the math and let you decide what the real returns have been and what you believe they might be in the future.

Macrotrends.net told us that the starting price of the Dow Jones Industrial Average (called the Dow) at the beginning of the twentieth century was $68. The same site found that the Dow closed one hundred years later at $11,457. Using a financial calculator, let's see if the math adds up:

Present value: $68
Future value: $11,457
Years: 100
Annual interest rate: 5.26 percent

What happened? Where did the advertised 12 percent go? What if the advertised number isn't reflective of the overall market growth?

At the time we write this book, it is nearing the end of 2021. Currently, the Dow sits at $34,500. Just twenty-one years ago, it was only $11,457. Is *that* a 12 percent return, as promised by Wall Street?

Let's take a look and see:

Present value: $11,457
Future value: $34,500
Years: 21
Annual Interest Rate: 5.39 percent

The point we're trying to make here is that the numbers advertised aren't aligning with the math.

VOLATILITY NOT MENTIONED

Think about how few people would participate in the whole stock market game if they knew the true statistics like the one mentioned above. If people could see that the Dow Jones was already falling short of its one-hundred-year anticipated average and it's only a quarter of the way through the century, what would they think? Would people be so quick to hand over their money?

Of course they wouldn't. But they are lured in through the percentages they read and by the ease of entry into the market. Wall Street marketers understand that most of us are busy and that we will take things at face value. So those advertised percentages make everyone think that their money can multiply without any energy exerted.

Have they mentioned the word *volatility* in their praise for the market? They should, because while they advertise one-hundred-year averages, what they fail to talk to you about is that your money typically only stays in the market for roughly forty years—from the time you enter the workforce and start investing until the time you leave it and tap into your retirement accounts.

Volatility can crush everything you've been working for. The wild swings up and down can make the market seem more like the gamble it is rather than a solid investment strategy. This becomes especially true when your entire retirement income becomes dependent upon what the stock market does during your time investing.

IT'S NOT ABOUT RETIREMENT

The idea for retirement started when people began living longer. In the late 1800s in Germany, Chancellor Otto von Bismarck came up with the idea to pay elderly people to leave the workforce. At the time, youth unemployment was on the rise and becoming a concern inside the country. So the idea seemed to be a good one—pay the elderly a retirement income so that they could leave the workforce, opening up jobs for others while still having an income to live on.

At the time, the age to qualify for this payment was seventy, but several years later, the age dropped to sixty-five, and worldwide, it hasn't budged much since then. But one thing has: the average life expectancy.

With people living longer after retirement, more money is being required. This is one of the primary reasons for retirement accounts being so heavily desired. There have been numerous studies on what amount of money can be withdrawn from a retirement account to insure that it doesn't go empty. The most notable is the 4 percent rule, which refers to the percentage of money that you can take out every year from your retirement account and have a 100 percent probability that your account will still have at least one dollar left in it at the end of twenty years.

Let's visualize this:

For every $40,000 in income, you need $1 million in your account. So if you make and spend $10,000 per month, you would need $3 million. Is that possible?

Joey has a perfect story that we both feel is far more common than people expect. While at the beach one day, wearing a Wealth Without Wall Street shirt, an elderly woman walked up to him and started asking him about it. Once she understood what the business was about and what we do, she said to Joey, "I worked forty years and saved a lot into my retirement account."

That was great, but let her next line to Joey that day sink in: "I just hope it's enough."

Forty years of saving and this woman was *still* worried that her retirement account might not last her long enough. She still had the fear that she would one day run out of money and have nothing.

The idea that a retirement account is a safety net couldn't be farther from the truth. The stock market is not your only option. You have many—you're just not seeing advertisements and being forced into these other options the way you are with the stock market.

That's why reading this book was such an important first step in your journey to Financial Freedom through passive income. Because passive income is what can allow you to know exactly where you stand in your goal to be financially free. When your passive income equals or exceeds your monthly expenses, you're financially free.

This process doesn't have to take forty years like the lady mentioned above. It is a process that can be obtained in a fraction of that time.

WHAT YOU NOW KNOW

We're not anti–Wall Street, we're pro-education. We believe in being educated on the income strategies you choose, and since Wall Street barely educates those whose money it takes, it's tough for us to get behind it. Mix that with the vast potential for exponential earnings through other areas and we're guided even farther away from that famed street in New York everyone is always mentioning.

This book reveals your alternatives. It is meant to provide insight and to guide you down paths that you might otherwise not be introduced to—paths that can truly change the trajectory of your life.

Wall Street seems to be the easy button. It's a way to throw your money into something and feel like it has earning potential. But instead of handing over your money and crossing your fingers, we have another option for you.

Put in ten hours per week for a few years. Educate yourself. Explore new avenues. Think about the things you would like to do and how you would like to make money well into your later years. Consider the alternatives that are mentioned in this book, in our community, and anywhere else you conduct your research.

More importantly, find your passion. Figure out what you're good at doing and start dedicating your time and energy toward learning about the framework that can lead you to financial success. Because only then will you be able to live that mailbox-money lifestyle where your only job is to walk out to the mailbox and collect checks.

Only then will you truly achieve Financial Freedom through passive income.

NEXT STEPS

The next step is to find that Support system. Before Wealth Without Wall Street, our Support came through the form of mentors—Nelson Nash, especially. When we started, our goal was to seek out the people who have had success in the areas we wanted to move into. It wasn't the simplest task in the world to reach out to all these people, which is why we have created a team of coaches right here at Wealth Without Wall Street for our community.

We created a Support system. Mentors from several investment areas who have had success in the past are now available to help those within our community. By reading this book, you have been opened up to the possibilities for passive income and a financially free life. But these ideas need to be put into practice, and our coaches can help do that without making the typical, first-timer mistakes.

What you can do from here is to pull together all the information you have taken from this book and discuss it with one of our coaches. With your completed Financial Passport in hand and insight from getting your Investor DNA, the next step gets clearer. You can schedule a free consultation with one of our coaches to determine your right next thing. You can do that at www.wealthwithoutwallstreet.com/book.

What happens from there? All we can tell you is that you are doing the one thing that will change your life: you take yet another step toward Financial Freedom.

CONCLUSION

Within these pages you have heard a lot of talk about money, and for good reason. Money is the means and the result of following the path laid out for you to gain Financial Freedom. However, money will never and can never be the end. Let us explain this a little further.

A few years back, we heard an interview with Tom Brady on ESPN. It was a little different than the typical interviews you hear when the person asking the questions makes the entire discussion about a game, or a play, or a look to the future for the star.

This one got deeper. In the interview, Tom shared things about his family and his personal life in addition to the customary talk about his career. The most interesting part of the interview came after Tom listed off the litany of things he had accomplished and the ridiculous wealth he had accumulated and his marriage to a supermodel, etc.

He ended the conversation with the statement, "Is this all there is?"

Imagine that for a second. If you could be in Tom Brady's

shoes for a minute, could you imagine ever saying those words? Wouldn't having all of those things be "enough" for you? We can assure you that whether you think you would find yourself saying it or not, the truth is this:

You would.

At the very base of Tom's statement is a longing and an emptiness he felt. Things, money, and fame will never ever satisfy that emptiness. Our desires are insatiable because they are placed within us all by an eternal God who fashioned each of us for a purpose. That purpose is not meant to serve ourselves. The blessings and knowledge and experiences and relationships He gives us are meant to be passed on and through each of us. Our purpose is to be in service to Him.

Sixteen hundred years ago, a man named Augustine said this in his classic book, *Confessions*: "Our hearts are restless until they find their rest in you." It is only when we surrender to that fact and put our hope and trust in God that we will cease striving to fill that void with things and prestige.

Here's our point: when you follow our process and gain Financial Freedom, it is our hope that you will be freed from the bondage of financial prison in order to truly pursue ways to impact and bless others with who you truly are. Until you break free of the financial chains you have been in, we believe you are limiting some of the ways you can be a blessing to others. If you embrace this mission, we believe people will see your good work and glorify God (Matthew 5:16).

We are on this mission, and this book is an outpouring of that vision. Will you join us? Will you steward the things you have been given in order to become financially free and continue to grow and develop into the person you were meant to be?

The two of us have not arrived. We continue to learn. If

we are anything, we are like beggars who are here to tell other beggars where we found the bread. By following *The Three Simple Steps to Freedom through Passive Income*, you too can impact your family, your community, and the world at large to honor God who gives such meaningful work to us.

Join us in the community and we would be honored to help you find your way down this path.

ACKNOWLEDGMENTS

There have been many people who have added to our journey and we fret to think of who will be left off this list.

To our parents, Joe, JoAnn, Bill, Barbara, Dorothy, Toby, and Suzie, for loving us and instilling a hard work ethic. To our wives, Jessica and Megan, who believed in us to go for it. To our children, Annie, Lily Kate, Chapel, Adler, Tyndall, Alexandria, Cate, Betsy, and Ryan, who inspired us to stop leaving for work and to find a way to come home. To Nelson Nash for waking us up to the problem and challenging us to think. To our many friends, colleagues, and peers in the financial world who shared insights and listened to our ideas: Jim Oliver, Anthony Faso, Cameron Christiansen, Caleb Guilliams, Tom Laune, Brent Kessler, Patrick Donohoe, Justin Craft, Joe Pantozzi, Mike Everett, Chris Bay, James Neathery, Jayson Lowe, Richard Canfield, David Stearns, Ray Poteet, Mary Jo Irmen, Ryan Lee, Brad Gibb, John Stewart, MC Laubscher, and Clay Hagler. To our coaches, consultants, and mentors who have helped us to dream bigger: Sharran Srivatsaa, Kitty Barrow, and Justin Harris. To Will Deshazo for nudging us to start a podcast. To the entire team at Wealth Without Wall Street, thank you for your amazing efforts to treat our company as your own. To Mark Podolsky for teaching us the land flipping business. To J. Massey for teaching us the short-term rental business. To Clint Lovette for helping us build our short-term rental empire and teaching our members how to do the same.

Thank you all for your contribution. We are humbled to know you all, and to call you friends.

ABOUT THE AUTHORS

 Wealth Without Wall Street's founder and partner **RUSS MORGAN** is known as "The Idea Guy." Russ began his professional career as an investment advisor in 2004 after graduating from Auburn University—a slight foray from ten-year-old Russ's dream of becoming a professional baseball pitcher. Russ started IBC in 2009, and eventually went on to found Wealth Without Wall Street in 2015. Russ's mother was an enormous inspiration for him growing up. As a single mother with two young children, she took a rigorous, accelerated track through college while working multiple jobs, all with the goal of bettering her children's lives. When he's not working, you can wave to Russ on a boat at the lake pulling his kids around on a tube. And on Sunday mornings, he's probably rushing to church with his family…only ten minutes late.

Russ's creativity, fresh ideas, and knack for problem-solving are indispensable assets to his role at Wealth Without Wall

Street. Russ would describe himself as competitive, creative, and passionate; his colleagues would likely add that he is helpful and abundant. Russ hopes to be remembered as an innovator who loved to teach others, and he has a goal to one day serve in the mission field. Finishing the book is another more near-term goal. Aside from Wealth Without Wall Street, Russ learns from the *Business School* podcast with Sharran Srivatsaa and Donald Miller's *Building a StoryBrand* book and podcast. Aspire Movement, Campus Outreach, and Young Business Leaders are three causes near to Russ's heart. Russ in one motto? "Just try!"

 **JOEY MURÉ**, Founder and Partner at Wealth Without Wall Street, brings impact, integrity, and generosity to the company every day. He hopes to be remembered as a lover of Jesus, devoted husband, and faithful father. Despite dreaming, around age ten, of becoming an orthopedic surgeon, Joey was in the mortgage business for eleven years before moving to finance in 2014. His personal mentor, Nelson Nash—another man of integrity and impact—is someone Joey deeply admires. Joey's strengths in building relationships, asking great questions, and influencing and empowering people with the Wealth Without Wall Street message make him invaluable to the company's mission. He is relational, impactful, and a true leader. His colleagues would add that he's thoughtful, funny, and a family man. Many people don't know that Joey ate a seventy-two-ounce steak dinner once. If he could be anywhere other than work, you'd find him at the beach with his family. And every Sunday morning, they're worshipping the Lord. A lifetime goal of Joey's is to impact the world for Christ, and a more near-term goal is to purchase a

beach house for his family. Aside from Wealth Without Wall Street, Joey listens to Sharran Srivatsaa's *Business School* podcast and Donald Miller's *Building a StoryBrand* podcast. He's happiest when he's traveling with his wife or golfing with his girls. He cares deeply about Campus Outreach, Cru, Navigators, Sav-a-Life, Lifeline Adoption, and Young Business Leaders. His aims is to live by the words "Trust in the Lord with all your heart and lean not on your own understanding. In all your ways acknowledge Him and He shall direct your path." (Proverbs 3:5–6)

Made in United States
Orlando, FL
07 June 2025

61904879R00113